MORE
Kids'
Favorite
BOOKS

A COMPILATION OF CHILDREN'S CHOICES 1992-1994

The Children's Book Council Inc.
568 Broadway
New York, NY 10012, USA

International Reading Association
800 Barksdale Road, PO Box 8139
Newark, DE 19714, USA

Children's Choices
A project of the International Reading Association
and the Children's Book Council

The Children's Book Council (CBC) is a nonprofit organization encouraging the reading and enjoyment of children's books. CBC sponsors National Children's Book Week each November and also prepares and sells display and informational materials to promote year-round reading. The Council cooperates on a variety of projects with the International Reading Association and with other national professional associations.

The International Reading Association is a nonprofit, professional organization of classroom teachers, reading specialists, administrators, educators of reading teachers, reading researchers, parents, librarians, psychologists, and others interested in improving reading instruction. It encourages study of the reading process, research, and better teacher education. It promotes the development of reading proficiency to the limit of each person's ability, an awareness of the need and importance of reading, and the formation of the reading habit.

The production of the three "Children's Choices" lists included in this book has involved many people in many different locations. In 1994 the International Reading Association/Children's Book Council joint committee responsible for organizing the project was chaired by Faye Johnston and Jeff Reynolds; test site team leaders were Betty Carter (Dallas/Fort Worth metroplex, TX); Carole Monlux (Missoula, MT); Rebecca Olness (Kent, WA); Dee Orth, Mary Hester, and Melinda Hodgson (Lyons, KS); and Phyllis Allen Smith (Marblehead, MA). Team leaders for 1993 were Doris Dillon (San Jose, CA), Karen Harris (New Orleans, LA), Rebecca Olness (Kent, WA), Phyllis Allen Smith (Marblehead, MA), and Ruth Walther (Belleville, IL). In 1992 team leaders were Doris Dillon (San Jose, CA), Karen Harris (New Orleans, LA), Rebecca Olness (Kent, WA), Adrienne Robb-Fund (Long Island, NY), and Ruth Walther (Belleville, IL). The joint committees for both 1992 and 1993 were chaired by Barbara Kiefer and Susan Pearson. CBC administrative staff coordinated the teams' work.

The lists included in this publication first appeared in *The Reading Teacher*, a copyrighted journal of the International Reading Association.

Contents

Introduction

Each year since 1975 the International Reading Association and the Children's Book Council have joined efforts to produce a list of about 100 titles that kids have chosen as their favorite books. Teachers, librarians, and parents look forward to receiving the new "Children's Choices" list each fall. The first list was published in 1975 in the Association's journal *The Reading Teacher*. A reprint of the list is also widely circulated each year.

The idea behind the list is simple. If children are to learn about the joy of reading and become proficient, lifelong readers, they need to know that books are fun. What better way to find books a child will like than to consult each year's version of Children's Choices, a list of titles selected by children themselves as "good reading"? The list can be used by anyone who is interested in children's reading material: teachers looking for titles to use in their classrooms, librarians and parents helping children choose special books for recreational reading, or friends and family hoping to find the perfect book to give as a gift. Children's Choices is organized by suggested reading levels to help in determining whether a particular book will be accessible to a particular child.

Although the idea behind the project is simple, the process by which each book is selected for inclusion in the list is elaborate. Each year approximately 500 new children's books (excluding textbooks) are sent to each of five test sites across the United States. At each of these sites, about 2,000 children participate in reading and evaluating the books. The children are asked "Do you like this book?" and get to vote "Yes," "No," or "Maybe." The votes from all five sites are tabulated, and the most popular books (usually just over 100 titles) are selected to appear as the year's Children's Choices. The coordinators of the project at the text sites determine whether the books are appropriate for All Ages, Beginning Independent Reading, Younger Readers (children approximately 5 to 8 years of age), Middle Grades (ages 8 to 10), or Older Readers (ages 10 to 13). The coordinators and their teams also prepare annotations for each title.

More Kids' Favorite Books lists the Children's Choices selections from 1992, 1993, and 1994—over 300 books in all. Each entry includes bibliographic information about the book and an annotation. (Please note that the publishers' names and the ISBNs refer to the original publication evaluated at the test sites. In some cases, paperback editions may now be available; in a few cases, the original edition may be difficult to find or unavailable. Librarians and bookstore employees should be able to provide current information on the availability of particular books. The intention in supplying the original bibliographic information is simply to provide a starting point.) To increase the collection's usefulness as a resource tool, we have included indexes of titles, authors, and illustrators.

More Kids' Favorite Books will make the job of finding the right book for the right child easy and fun. And because these books were chosen by children themselves, reading a Children's Choices book will likely show children that reading can be easy and fun, too!

All Ages

An Alphabet of Rotten Kids!

David Elliott. Illustrated by Oscar de Mejo. Philomel. ISBN 0-399-22260-X. CC '92.

> The alphabet will never seem the same after you read this book! Meet Horatio, who stuffs his mouth with frozen peas then sneezes! And meet Bartholomew, who pours ink into his teacher's tea and turns her lips blue. These 26 poems are about some of the most rotten, mischievous, uncontrollable children you'll ever meet. The students will love them.

Amanda's Perfect Hair

Linda Milstein. Illustrated by Susan Meddaugh. Tambourine. ISBN 0-688-11153-X. CC '94.

> Amanda has the longest, thickest, curliest, most beautiful hair in the world. Everybody says so. But Amanda thinks people care only about her hair and sets out to show them what a special person she really is.

And the Green Grass Grew All Around: Folk Poetry from Everyone

Collected by Alvin Schwartz. Illustrated by Sue Truesdell. HarperCollins. ISBN 0-06-022757-5. CC '93.

> Children will love chanting, singing, and jumping rope to this humorous treasury representing the backbone of American folk poetry. The book is a "must have" for the child in all of us! Understand, rubber band?

The Australian Echidna

Eleanor Stodart. Illustrated with color photographs.
Houghton Mifflin. ISBN 0-395-55992-8. CC '92.

> The life cycle of the amazing and unusual Australian echidna,
> or anteater, is told with an easily understandable, fact-filled
> text and over 40 dramatic color photographs!

Belly's Deli

R.L. Shafner and Eric Jon Weisberg. Illustrated by Nancy
Bauer. Lerner. ISBN 0-8225-2101-6. CC '94.

> Why is so much food disappearing from Belly's Deli? This
> book takes you on a pun-filled adventure in search of the
> thief. You'll relish the excitement Belly feels when he's
> finally able to ketchup with the thief.

The Big Green Book

Fred Pearce. Illustrated by Ian Winton. Grosset & Dunlap.
ISBN 0-448-40142-8. CC '92.

> Realistic, factual, and thorough, this book uses catchy chap-
> ter titles but a matter-of-fact tone to show how humans affect
> the earth, especially today. Included is a list of books, maga-
> zines, and organizations that tell us "what we need to help our
> Earth."

Birds: A First Discovery Book

Created by Gallimard Jeunesse, Claude Delafosse, and René
Mettler. Illustrated by René Mettler. Scholastic. ISBN 0-590-
46367-5. CC '94.

> See a skeleton beneath the feathers of a bird. Discover a nest
> of eggs hidden in a tree. Watch a ptarmigan change colors
> with the changing seasons. Illustrated transparent overlays
> add to the beauty of this innovative approach to nonfiction.
> Originally published in France in 1990 by Editions Galli-
> mard.

Illustration by Patricia Polacco from her Chicken Sunday. *©1992 by Patricia Polacco. Reprinted by permission of Philomel Books.*

Chicken Sunday
Patricia Polacco. Illustrated by the author. Philomel. ISBN 399-22133-6. CC '93.

> Patricia Polacco invites the reader to her old neighborhood by sharing a wonderful story of acceptance, trust, and love. Her story comes to life in her vibrant colors and folk-art style.

The Children's Animal Atlas
David Lambert. Millbrook. ISBN 1-56294-101-1. CC '93.

> Oversized, colorful, and well organized from the five-section contents to the index, this atlas includes maps, pictures, charts, and text with information ready for discovery. The book may be savored like a good novel or explored by sections.

Children's Classics to Read Aloud
Selected by Edward Blishen. Illustrated in color and black and white. Kingfisher Books. ISBN 1-85697-825-7. CC '93.

> This collection of excerpts from 20 exciting, dramatic, adventurous, suspenseful, and humorous books provides children with wonderful read-aloud stories. Approximate reading times and skills for reading aloud are included.

Christmas in July
Arthur Yorinks. Illustrated by Richard Egielski. HarperCollins. ISBN 0-06-020257-2. CC '92.

> Townspeople were prepared for Santa's visit. However, Santa was unable to make his deliveries because his pants were lost at the dry cleaners. Santa's attempts to rescue his pants make a good, comical Christmas read. A second grader exclaimed, "This book should get a 10!"

Cinderella
Retold by William Wegman with Carole Kismaric and Marvin Heiferman. Illustrated with photographs by William Wegman. Hyperion. ISBN 1-56282-348-5. CC '94.

> A true classic presented in a refreshing way, using dogs as the main characters and other animals in supporting roles. The dazzling photographs and visual interpretation renew the spirit of *Cinderella*, making it a story for all ages. A first grader remarked, "It was so funny!"

The Frog Prince Continued
Jon Scieszka. Illustrated by Steve Johnson. Viking. ISBN 0-670-83421-1. CC '92.

> A delightful and humorous sequel in which the Prince and Princess find out the shocking truth about life "happily ever after." All ages will enjoy this book.

From Sea to Shining Sea: A Treasury of American Folklore and Folk Songs

Compiled by Amy L. Cohn. Illustrated by Molly Bang, Marcia Brown, Barbara Cooney, Donald Crews, Leo Dillon, Diane Dillon, Richard Egielski, Trina Schart Hyman, Anita Lobel, Jerry Pinkney, John Schoenherr, Marc Simont, Chris Van Allsburg, David Wiesner, and Ed Young. Scholastic. ISBN 0-590-42868-3. CC '94.

> Enhanced by the illustrations of Caldecott artists, this thematic collection of folklore, poems, songs, and essays celebrates the diversity of American heritage and belongs in every American classroom.

Gobble! The Complete Book of Thanksgiving Words

Lynda Graham-Barber. Illustrated by Betsy Lewin. Bradbury. ISBN 0-02-708332-2. CC '92.

> "A book for fun and information" wrote one seventh grader. Each custom or food related to Thanksgiving is explored in detail. An American history trivia book.

Gonna Sing My Head Off!

Collected and arranged by Kathleen Krull. Illustrated by Allen Garns. Knopf. ISBN 0-394-81991-8. CC '93.

> This collection of 62 of America's best-loved folk songs is a tribute to American music. Beautifully illustrated, this book includes music for both piano and guitar along with historical headnotes and an introduction by Arlo Guthrie.

Good Days, Bad Days: An Official NFL Book

Edited by Tom Barnidge. Illustrated with full-color photographs. Viking. ISBN 0-670-84686-4. CC '93.

> Even super athletes have bad days, and lessons can be learned from these stories of determination, embarrassment, victory, and defeat. Children are heavily influenced by professional football players, and inspiration is in heavy supply here.

Hey, Hay! A Wagonful of Funny Homonym Riddles

Marvin Terban. Illustrated by Kevin Hawkes. Clarion. ISBN 0-395-54431-9. CC '92.

> "These riddles are fun!" exclaimed a third grader when this homonym riddle book was read aloud. The answers are all homonyms—sometimes two, three, and even four words that sound the same.

Hidden Pictures

Linda Bolton. Dial. ISBN 0-8037-1378-9. CC '94.

> An intriguing book that opens up new ways of looking at art. It may be enjoyed alone, but it is too good not to share with someone.

Hiding Out: Camouflage in the Wild

James Martin. Photographs by Art Wolfe. Crown. ISBN 0-517-59392-0. CC '94.

> From the orchid mantis to the Kenyan sand boa, camouflage is a means of survival. Throughout Martin's book, beautiful photographs demonstrate the art of disguise. Readers of all ages are sure to find it fascinating!

I Am Really a Princess

Carol Diggory Shields. Illustrated by Paul Meisel. Dutton. ISBN 0-525-45138-2. CC '94.

> Kids of all ages have probably wondered what life would be like with a King and Queen as parents. A delightful tale of a girl determined that in real life she is a princess.

Incredible Cross-Sections

Richard Platt. Illustrated by Stephen Biesty. Knopf. ISBN 0-679-81411-6. CC '93.

> Students experience X-ray vision in this meticulously illustrated presentation of the inner workings of 18 complex vehicles and buildings from the past and present. Biesty's cutaway drawings expose the intricacies of a medieval castle, and children can explore mysteries inside the space shuttle. On

two special pages, the drawing of an ocean liner and a steam train fold open to 3 feet.

It Was a Dark and Stormy Night
Keith Moseley. Illustrated by Linda Birkinshaw. Dial. ISBN 0-8037-1021-6. CC '92.

> Lady Penelope is having a party to show off her new treasure, the Dudley Diamond. The lights go out and the diamond is stolen! Who took it? A great whodunit mystery with pop-up pictures.

Jack and the Beanstalk
Retold by Steven Kellogg. Illustrated by the author. Morrow. ISBN 0-688-10250-6. CC '92.

> This rich retelling of the popular tale, featuring Kellogg's magical, often humorous illustrations, has universal appeal. As one class commented, "We think Mr. Kellogg is a great artist."

Jane Yolen's Mother Goose Songbook
Selected, edited, and introduced by Jane Yolen. Illustrated by Rosekrans Hoffman. Boyds Mills Press. ISBN 1-878093-52-5. CC '93.

> Children know and love these popular rhymes. The brief introduction before each tune will encourage the reader to continue through the book. The simple musical arrangements will enable parents, teachers, and children to play and sing along.

The Kingfisher Children's Encyclopedia
Edited by John Paton. Illustrated with over 2,000 color illustrations, photographs, and maps. Kingfisher Books. ISBN 1-85697-800-1. CC '93.

> Children and young adults will enjoy browsing through more than 1,300 carefully selected topics that are alphabetically arranged, cross referenced, and skillfully illustrated with full-color artwork and photography. The entries are up-to-date and relevant for today's young readers.

Knock! Knock!
Colin and Jacqui Hawkins. Illustrated by Colin Hawkins.
Aladdin. ISBN 0-689-71475-0. CC '92.

> "Who's there?" or "What's there?" Thrills, chills, and laughter
> await readers of all ages as they guess what creature lurks be-
> hind the door.

Making Books: A Step-By-Step Guide to Your Own Publishing
Gillian Chapman and Pam Robson. Illustrated with photographs. Millbrook. ISBN 1-56294-169-0. CC '93.

> A gold mine of ideas for helping students plan, design, and
> make their own books. Booklets, scrolls, bound books, and
> pop-up books, as well as lettering, marbling, and printing are
> beautifully explained and illustrated. "It was so neat, I'm
> making my own book," wrote one 3rd grader. "I must have
> this book!" was the comment of another student.

Making Tracks: A Slide-and-See Book
Stephen Savage. Illustrated by the author. Lodestar. ISBN 0-
525-67353-9. CC '93.

> This "slide and see" book will attract children of all ages.
> Readers will be delighted to discover an animal in its natural
> environment by manipulating a pull-out tab to see its foot-
> print.

The Man Behind the Magic: The Story of Walt Disney
Katherine and Richard Greene. Illustrated with photographs.
Viking. ISBN 0-670-82259-0. CC '92.

> Walt Disney was not afraid to work hard and make his
> dreams become a reality. This book contains many interest-
> ing quotes by Disney and is a very descriptive biography.

Martha Speaks

Susan Meddaugh. Illustrated by the author. Houghton
Mifflin. ISBN 0-395-63313-3. CC '93.

> Children love Martha, a dog who not only speaks but speaks
> her mind. Martha must learn to curb her endless chatter and
> her sometimes hurtful, albeit truthful, comments. The cartoon-
> like illustrations with the dialogue in a balloon add to the
> fun.

Mistakes That Worked

Charlotte Foltz Jones. Illustrated by John O'Brien. Doubleday.
ISBN 0-385-26246-9. CC '92.

> Tells the who, what, where, when, and how of things we use
> each day that started out as mistakes, such as doughnut holes,
> Popsicles, and Coca-Cola. Kids learn that making a mistake is
> a learning experience.

Monster Mama

Liz Rosenberg. Illustrated by Stephen Gammell. Philomel.
ISBN 0-399-21989-7. CC '94.

> Patrick Edward's mother is sweet, tender, and very protective,
> but she also lives in a cave and has magic powers. Gammell's
> illustrations create a surreal mood for the boy's adventures.

Mrs. Bretsky's Bakery

R.L. Shafner and Eric Jon Weisberg. Illustrated by Nancy
Bauer. Lerner. ISBN 0-8225-2102-4. CC '94.

> Puns of fun is what you'll feel when reading Mrs. Bretsky's
> Bakery. Readers of all ages will rise to the occasion and agree
> that this book takes the cake!

Nature's Deadly Creatures: A Pop-Up Exploration

Frances Jones. Illustrated by Tony Smith and Andrew
Robinson. Dial. ISBN 0-8037-1342-8. CC '93.

> "Fascinating" describes this pop-up book about venomous an-
> imals such as the scorpion, blue-ringed octopus, Gila mon-
> ster, cobra snake, black widow spider, and zebrafish. Cleverly
> designed to look lifelike, each entry also opens in a side panel
> with much written and graphic detail.

Not the Piano, Mrs. Medley!

Evan Levine. Illustrated by S.D. Schindler. Orchard. ISBN 0-
531-05956-1. CC '92.

> "It's like my Mom camping," commented one young child.
> Mrs. Medley just can't seem to leave anything at home as she
> prepares to go to the beach. Once at the seashore, she forgets
> all about those "necessities."

Old Black Fly

Jim Aylesworth. Illustrated by Stephen Gammell. Holt. ISBN
0-8050-1401-2. CC '93.

> Learning the alphabet isn't boring! Especially when taught
> with the help of an annoying old, black fly. With the use of

repetition and hilarious illustrations, children will quickly join in the fun of reading this book. The ending is smashing!

The Old Ladies Who Liked Cats

Carol Greene. Illustrated by Loretta Krupinski. HarperCollins. ISBN 0-06-022104-6. CC '92.

> Mutual need is the theme of this book that describes how some old ladies saved the town by letting their cats out at night. This funny story deals with the balance of nature and will be enjoyed by all.

175 Amazing Nature Experiments

Rosie Harlow and Gareth Morgan. Illustrated by Kuo Kang Chen and others. Random House. ISBN 0-679-82043-4. CC '93.

> This book contains a wonderful collection of simple science experiments that help explain how nature works. Using commonly found materials, children or a child and adult can do hands-on investigations of plants, the seasons, insects, worms, and snails.

Parents in the Pigpen, Pigs in the Tub

Amy Ehrlich. Illustrated by Steven Kellogg. Dial. ISBN 0-8037-0933-1. CC '94.

> This is a delightful book about a crazy swap between people and barnyard animals. Kellogg's zany illustrations combined with Ehrlich's tongue-in-cheek dialogue will charge the imaginations of young and old alike.

Planes of the Aces: A Three-Dimensional Collection of the Most Famous Aircraft in the World

Joan Bowden. Illustrated by Stef Suchomski. Doubleday/Bantam Doubleday Dell. ISBN 0-385-30910-4. CC '94.

> In this book for airplane enthusiasts, historical and statistical facts accompany seven three-dimensional pop-up planes, ranging from the Red Baron's World War I Fokker to the Tornado GR.1, which flew in the Persian Gulf War.

Somebody Catch My Homework

David L. Harrison. Illustrated by Betsy Lewin. Boyds Mills Press. ISBN 1-878093-87-8. CC '94.

> Original and humorous poems about school experiences include the agony of homework and tests, the horrors of cafeteria food, the classroom bully, and the joy of reading your very first book.

Somebody Loves You, Mr. Hatch

Eileen Spinelli. Illustrated by Paul Yalowitz. Bradbury. ISBN 0-02-786015-9. CC '92.

> A sad and lonely man becomes enlightened when a special gift is sent to him. This story shows the importance of friendship in everyone's life.

A Southern Time Christmas

Robert Bernardini. Illustrated by James Rice. Pelican. ISBN 0-88289-828-0. CC '92.

> Students enjoy this hilarious regional take-off on the traditional Christmas poem "The Night Before Christmas." Jed, Santa's elf, gives special insights into customs that are uniquely Southern. A good read-aloud.

The Stinky Cheese Man and Other Fairly Stupid Tales

Jon Scieszka. Illustrated by Lane Smith. Viking. ISBN 0-670-84487-X. CC '93.

> Scieszka and Smith are again poking fun at the traditional folk tales we know and love. They even wreak havoc with the title page, table of contents, and ISBN. A hit with all ages.

The Story in a Picture: Children in Art

Robin Richmond. Illustrated with fine art from around the world. Ideals Publishing Corp. ISBN 0-8249-8552-4. CC '93.

> In this wonderful reference book with a new approach to looking at art, Robin Richmond tries to describe the picture

and help us understand what the artist is trying to express. We learn art history as well as art appreciation.

Tailypo!
Retold by Jan Wahl. Illustrated by Wil Clay. Holt. ISBN 0-8050-0687-7. CC '92.

> A wonderful African-American folk-tale told by an old man to the author: Why never to chase with a hatchet a creature that has a long, long tail and is crawling through your wall!

Talking with Artists
Compiled and edited by Pat Cummings. Illustrated in full-color and black-and-white photographs. Bradbury Press. ISBN 0-02-724245-5. CC '93.

> Fourteen distinguished children's book illustrators talk about their early art experiences and answer questions frequently asked by students. Also of interest are photographs of the artists and samples of their artwork both as children and adults.

Tyrannosaurus
William Lindsay. Illustrated with photographs. Dorling Kindersley. ISBN 1-56458-124-1. CC '94.

> This thorough reference book with dramatic photographs of realistic models from the American Museum of Natural History details the discovery and excavation, reconstruction, and location of the world's most ferocious dinosaur.

Voices of the Wild
Jonathan London. Illustrated by Wayne McLoughlin. Crown. ISBN 0-517-59217-7. CC '94.

> This beautifully illustrated book details messages of nature as seen through the eyes of animals. Readers will be inspired by the animals' simple observations of the need for balance in nature.

Walt Disney's 101 Dalmatians: Illustrated Classic

Adapted from the film by Ann Braybrooks. Illustrated by Gil DiCicco. Disney. ISBN 1-56282-010-9. CC '92.

> Newlywed Dalmatians and their human "pets" take you on an adventure as their family stretches from 15 puppies to a plantation for 101 Dalmatians. This story is filled with suspense and beautiful illustrations. A book to be shared by the whole family.

Whales

Gail Gibbons. Illustrated by the author. Holiday House. ISBN 0-8234-0900-7. CC '92.

> This well illustrated, factual book on the lives of many different whales easily piques curiosity and raises questions for discussion. "I didn't know...." is a comment often heard.

When I Was Your Age

Ken Adams. Illustrated by Val Biro. Barron's. ISBN 0-8120-6249-3. CC '92.

> "That's just what my Grandpa says!" was one comment overheard when a teacher read aloud this delightful book about Sammy and his boastful grandpa, who had things much worse when he was a boy. Val Biro's illustrations are hilarious.

The Willow Pattern Story

Allan Drummond. Illustrated by the author. North-South Books. ISBN 1-55858-171-5. CC '93.

> The author uses a story told to him as a child as he explains the mystery of the blue willow pottery design. Drummond takes the reader on a wonderful adventure about two Chinese lovers punished by one's cruel Mandarin father.

Wind in the Long Grass: A Collection of Haiku

Edited by William J. Higginson. Illustrated by Sandra Speidel. Simon & Schuster. ISBN 0-671-67978-3. CC '92.

> An international collection with illustrations as gently evocative as haiku itself. Children commented, "The beautiful pictures make me feel peaceful." A brief description of haiku's structure encourages youngsters to try their hand at this ancient poetic form.

Window on the Deep: The Adventures of Underwater Explorer Sylvia Earle

Andrea Conley. Illustrated with photographs. Franklin Watts. ISBN 0-531-15232-4. CC '92.

> This book is a wonderful way to learn about scuba diving and ocean life. Beautiful photographs and detailed illustrations.

A Young Painter: The Life and Paintings of Wang Yani—China's Extraordinary Young Artist

Zheng Zhensun and Alice Low. Illustrated with photographs and reproductions. Scholastic. ISBN 0-590-44906-0. CC '92.

> The life and works of Wang Yani, a Chinese girl who started painting at age 3 in China. Many beautiful color photographs of her monkeys, lions, cranes, peacocks, and landscape paintings.

Beginning
Independent
Reading

Big Pumpkin
Erica Silverman. Illustrated by S.D. Schindler. Macmillan.
ISBN 0-02-782683-X. CC '93.

> A predictable Halloween story that proves cooperation is
> valuable. The witch wants pumpkin pie for Halloween but
> can't get the big pumpkin off the vine. Various monsters offer
> help and suggestions. Repetition makes this a delightful story.

The Cut-Ups Crack Up
James Marshall. Illustrated by the author. Viking. ISBN 0-670-
84486-1. CC '93.

> Young readers take great pleasure in sharing the humorously
> written and illustrated stories by James Marshall. This latest
> in the Cut-Ups series is no exception. Children share zany
> adventures as Spud and Joe borrow their school principal's
> sports car and take it for a joyride. As one first grader asked
> another excitedly, "Where would you take the car if you had
> the chance?"

Draw Me a Star

Eric Carle. Illustrated by the author. Philomel. ISBN 399-
21877-7. CC '93.

> Eric Carle's simple text and drawings can be an inspiration to
> young writers and illustrators. He shows us how a story can
> begin with a simple object like a star, develop into a story,
> and end with the same simple object.

Easy to See Why

Fred Gwynne. Illustrated by the author. Simon & Schuster.
ISBN 0-671-79776-X. CC '94.

> This humorous, easy-to-read rhyming story about a dog show
> is accompanied by pictures of dogs and their look-alike own-
> ers. The twist at the end will leave all mutt owners feeling
> that, indeed, the right dog won!

Five Little Monkeys Sitting in a Tree

Eileen Christelow. Illustrated by the author. Clarion. ISBN 0-
395-54434-3. CC '92.

> A humorous, familiar tale of five monkeys who tease a croco-
> dile. One second grader commented, "It's good because it
> repeats, and you get to know the words."

Illustration from The Giant Zucchini *by Catherine Siracusa* ©1993.
Reprinted by permission of Hyperion Books for Children.

The Giant Zucchini
Catherine Siracusa. Illustrated by the author. Hyperion. ISBN
1-56282-286-1. CC '94.

> The giant zucchini seed grew only one teeny zucchini. What
> a surprise when Edgar and Robert started singing and the
> zucchini started growing! The surprises don't end there; this
> book is imaginative, funny, and a delight to read aloud.

The Happy Hippopotami
Bill Martin Jr. Illustrated by Betsy Everitt. HBJ. ISBN 0-15-
233380-0. CC '92.

> A happy-hippo adventure to the beach is filled with colorful
> pictures and creative language that invite the reader to par-
> ticipate. You will want to join the hilarious hippopotami for a
> hip-hippo celebration next year.

Happy Thanksgiving Rebus

David A. Adler. Illustrated by Jan Palmer. Viking. ISBN 0-670-83388-6. CC '92.

> This story within a story is enriched by rebus pictures and detailed illustrations. The story of the first Thanksgiving helps a modern boy learn the real meaning of sharing.

How Do You Say It Today, Jesse Bear?

Nancy White Carlstrom. Illustrated by Bruce Degen. Macmillan. ISBN 0-02-717276-7. CC '93.

> In this fourth book about a lovable little bear, Jesse Bear has his own special way of saying "I love you" every month of the year. A colorful celebration of holidays and seasons in rhyme.

From How Do You Say It Today, Jesse Bear? *by Nancy White Carlstrom. Illustration ©1992 by Bruce Degen. Reprinted by permission of the Simon & Schuster Children's Publishing Division.*

If Dinosaurs Came to Town

Dom Mansell. Illustrated by the author. Little, Brown. ISBN 0-316-54584-8. CC '92.

> What would it be like if dinosaurs were still alive and roaming around your town? What would they be like? Where would they live? Would you be safe? Read this book and you'll find out!

In a Cabin in a Wood

Adapted by Darcie McNally. Illustrated by Robin Michal Koontz. Cobblehill. ISBN 0-525-65035-0. CC '92.

> A colorful story from the song "In a Cabin in a Wood." A rabbit comes up with a clever solution that helps an old man. Very detailed illustrations.

In the Tall, Tall Grass

Denise Fleming. Illustrated by the author. Holt. ISBN 0-8050-1635-X. CC '92.

> Catchy, rhyming words in big print skip and dip across the pages of this read-aloud book. It is a book to share, with bright illustrations that reveal insects and grassy creatures. Children ask, "What's next?"

Matthew's Dream

Leo Lionni. Illustrated by the author. Knopf. ISBN 0-679-81075-7. CC '92.

> Matthew doesn't know what he wants to be when he grows up. A trip to the museum helps him decide, and his dreary world becomes bright and colorful.

Monkey Soup

Louis Sachar. Illustrated by Cat Bowman Smith. Knopf. ISBN 0-679-80297-5. CC '92.

> Monkey soup is a hilarious new cure for a cold, according to a young daughter. When Daddy has the sniffles, she concocts a soup with all the things that make her feel better when she is ill.

My Friend Whale
Simon James. Illustrated by the author. Bantam. ISBN 0-553-07065-7. CC '92.

> Simple words and delightful pictures tell the story of a boy's friendship with a blue whale. Along the way, the reader learns facts about whales and their fragile environment.

Piggies
Don Wood and Audrey Wood. Illustrated by Don Wood. HBJ. ISBN 0-15-256341-5. CC '92.

> Here is a new twist on "This Little Piggy Goes to Market." The Woods have red little pigs on 10 fingers, and the pigs are fat, smart, long, silly, and wee. They are usually good, but at bedtime they dance on your toes.

Seven Blind Mice
Ed Young. Illustrated by the author. Philomel. ISBN 399-22261-8. CC '92.

> A good learning book for the young reader, the story incorporates the lessons of colors, numbers, and the days of the week. It also teaches the moral lessons of patience and of making a full investigation before coming to a conclusion.

Sheep in a Shop
Nancy Shaw. Illustrated by Margot Apple. Houghton Mifflin. ISBN 0-395-53681-2. CC '92.

> Can you imagine seeing some silly sheep on a birthday shopping spree with no money? This wonderfully illustrated book sheds some "shear" delight on a silly, sheepish solution to their problem.

Illustration from Sheep in a Shop *by Nancy Shaw. Illustrations ©1991 by Margot Apple. Reprinted by permission of Houghton Mifflin Company. All rights reserved.*

Sheep Out To Eat

Nancy Shaw. Illustrated by Margot Apple. Houghton Mifflin. ISBN 0-395-61128-8. CC '92.

> Young readers enjoyed the sheep's latest hilarious adventures, this time in a restaurant. The easy-to-read rhyming text and humorous illustrations appeal to children again and again. As one first grader exclaimed, "I can't wait to see what kind of trouble the sheep get into this time!"

Super Cluck

Jane O'Connor and Robert O'Connor. Illustrated by Megan Lloyd. HarperCollins. ISBN 0-06-24594-8. CC '92.

> A big strong chick from another planet has trouble making friends with the other chickens, but during a heroic act he proves he is not a wimpy or dumb chick after all.

Trade-in Mother

Marisabina Russo. Illustrated by the author. Greenwillow. ISBN 0-688-11416-4. CC '94.

> Max's day starts with a smile but ends with a frown. Young readers relate to Max's desires and frustrations as well as his resolutions to problems. Detailed illustrations enhance the eventful story.

Walt Disney's 101 Dalmatians: A Counting Book

Fran Manushkin. Illustrated by Russell Hicks. Disney. ISBN 1-56282-012-5. CC '92.

> Out for a walk, 99 puppies are frightened by a fire truck and run in all directions. Young readers count from 1 to 101 while finding the missing puppies on each page. A real favorite of kindergartners and first graders.

When I Was Little: A Four-Year-Old's Memoir of Her Youth

Jamie Lee Curtis. Illustrated by Laura Cornell. HarperCollins. ISBN 0-06-021078-8. CC '94.

> A girl tells about her life as a baby and compares it to being 4 years old. The repetitive, simple words help young readers enjoy this book, yet the text and illustrations make humorous reading for all ages.

Younger Readers

Alamo Across Texas
Jill Stover. Illustrated by the author. Lothrop, Lee & Shepard.
ISBN 0-688-11712-0. CC '94.

> When a drought comes to the Lavaca River area, Alamo the
> alligator searches for a new home. Simple repetitive text ac-
> companies colorful illustrations as Alamo treks across Texas.

An Alligator Named...Alligator
Lois G. Grambling. Illustrated by Doug Cushman. Barron's.
ISBN 0-8120-6224-8. CC '92.

> A little boy's desire for a pet alligator turns into an unusual
> surprise for his family and neighbors. What do you do with an
> alligator in the house?

Anansi Goes Fishing
Retold by Eric A. Kimmel. Illustrated by Janet Stevens.
Holiday House. ISBN 0-8234-0918-X. CC '92.

> A companion volume to *Anansi and the Moss-Covered Rock*,
> this is a laugh-filled tale of lazy Anansi the Spider, who tries
> to trick his friend Turtle into catching fish for him. But poor
> Anansi's plan backfires!

Andrew's Amazing Monsters

Kathryn Hook Berlan. Illustrated by Maxie Chambliss. Atheneum. ISBN 0-689-31739-5. CC '94.

> Andrew loves monsters and covers his walls with monster pictures. He wishes he could give them a party, and one night Andrew has a wonderful surprise.

Andrew Wants a Dog

Steven Kroll. Illustrated by Molly Delaney. Hyperion. ISBN 1-56282-118-0. CC '92.

> This is a delightful story about a boy named Andrew who wants a dog more than anything. Unfortunately, Andrew's father does not like dogs. After many unsuccessful attempts to change dad's mind, Andrew disguises himself as a dog. When his parents find him on their doorstep, they see they do like dogs.

From Andrew's Amazing Monsters *by Kathryn H. Berlan. Illustrations ©1993 by Maxie Chambliss. Courtesy Atheneum Books for Young Readers, an imprint of Simon & Schuster Children's Publishing Division.*

Appalachia? The Voices of Sleeping Birds

Cynthia Rylant. Illustrated by Barry Moser. HBJ. ISBN 0-15-201605-8. CC '92.

> This is an easy-to-read book about the Appalachian Mountain people growing up and living in coal mining areas.

Arthur Babysits

Marc Brown. Illustrated by the author. Joy Street/Little, Brown. ISBN 0-316-11293-3. CC '92.

> Young readers loved Arthur's newest adventure, babysitting for "the terrible Tibble twins." It turns out to be a night to remember, as Arthur outwits the mischievous twins with tricks, laughter, and storytime fun.

Arthur Meets the President

Marc Brown. Illustrated by the author. Joy Street/Little, Brown. ISBN 0-316-11265-8. CC '92.

> Arthur wins an essay contest and is off with his classmates to attend a ceremony at the White House. When Arthur forgets his speech, he gets some unexpected help in this 15th book in the humorous Arthur Adventure series.

Arthur's Family Vacation

Marc Brown. Illustrated by the author. Little, Brown. ISBN 0-316-11312-3. CC '94.

> Arthur wants to go to camp with his friend but has to go to the beach with his family instead, where it rains for days! Then Arthur creates rainy day field trips for the family and rescues their vacation.

Aunt Elaine Does the Dance from Spain

Leah Komaiko. Illustrated by Petra Mathers. Bantam Doubleday Dell. ISBN 0-385-30674-1. CC '92.

> Little Katy is so surprised to see what happens to her Aunt Elaine when she dons her Spanish costume and takes the stage. The rhythms and Spanish vocabulary lead you through the book and enhance the illustrations. Ole!

Aunt Isabel Tells a Good One

Kate Duke. Illustrated by the author. Dutton. ISBN 0-525-44835-7. CC '92.

> Little Penelope wants a bedtime story. Aunt Isabel explains, "A good story is the hardest kind to tell. We must put it together carefully, with just the right ingredients." Using basic story grammar, the two concoct an exciting tale within their own story—demonstrating writing elements that even the youngest readers can understand.

The Bathwater Gang Gets Down to Business: A Springboard Book

Jerry Spinelli. Illustrated by Meredith Johnson. Little, Brown. ISBN 0-316-80808-3. CC '92.

> Can the Bathwater Gang earn enough money to go to the circus? Bertie thinks they can by running a pet washing business, but things don't run as smoothly as they anticipate. Will Bertie's bright idea to increase business help or hurt them?

The Bear That Heard Crying

Natalie Kinsey-Warnock and Helen Kinsey. Illustrated by Ted Rand. Cobblehill. ISBN 0-525-65103-9. CC '94.

> Three-year-old Sarah, lost in the woods, snuggles up to a big black "dog." Exciting text and illustrations make for independent reading or reading aloud with many chances for prediction and discussion.

Benjamin Bigfoot

Mary Serfozo. Illustrated by Jos. A. Smith. Margaret K. McElderry Books. ISBN 0-689-50570-1. CC '94.

> If you were an eager 5-year-old heading off to school for the very first time, how could you make yourself bigger? Small children will identify with Benjamin's concerns about beginning school.

From The Bathwater Gang Gets Down to Business *by Jerry Spinelli.*
Text ©1992 by Jerry Spinelli; illustrations ©1992 by Meridith Johnson.
By permission of Little, Brown and Company.

Brown Bear, Brown Bear, What Do You See?
(25th Anniversary Edition)
Bill Martin Jr. Illustrated by Eric Carle. ISBN 0-8050-1744-5.
CC '92.

> Even after 25 years, kindergarten children are still captivated by the bold and striking illustrations of Eric Carle and the predictable, read-along rhyme of Bill Martin Jr. This new edition of a favorite classic is a crowd pleaser.

Calico Cows
Arlene Dubanevich. Illustrated by the author. Viking. ISBN 0-670-84436-5. CC '94.

> These are "cool calico cows" wrote one youngster responding to this story of a herd of multicolored bovines who temporarily lose their leader and have to cope with the day's activities on their own.

Castles: A First Discovery Book
Created by Gallimard Jeunesse, Claude Delafosse, and C. & D. Millet. Illustrated by C. & D. Millet. Scholastic. ISBN 0-590-46377-2. CC '94.

> Inviting! A brief, readable introduction to medieval castles and the daily life of people who lived there. Bright illustrations using transparent overlays "picture the text." Some information on knights is also included. Originally published in France in 1990 by Editions Gallimard.

The Christmas Witch
Steven Kellogg. Illustrated by the author. Dial. ISBN 0-8037-1268-5. CC '92.

> This is a delightful tale of how a little witch named Gloria brings the joy and friendship of the Christmas spirit to the feuding communities of the Pepperwills and the Valdoons. This is a wonderful story of how good triumphs over evil.

Christopher Columbus: From Vision to Voyage

Joan Anderson. Illustrated with photographs by George Ancona. Dial. ISBN 0-8037-1041-0. CC '92.

> Columbus, an ordinary man who had the sea in his veins and dreams in his head, changed people's view of the world forever. Anderson and Ancona bring history to life as they reveal the inner journey that led to Columbus's first sailing in 1492.

Cinderella Penguin

Retold by Janet Perlman. Illustrated by Janet Perlman. Viking. ISBN 0-670-84753-4. CC '94.

> An appealing heroine, a handsome prince, and a glass flipper add sly humor to this familiar fairy tale starring penguins rather than humans.

Clifford, We Love You

Norman Bridwell. Illustrated by the author. Scholastic. ISBN 0-590-43843-3. CC '92.

> Emily Elizabeth and her big red dog Clifford have delighted boys and girls for 25 years, but now Clifford feels blue. Nothing can cheer him until Emily Elizabeth decides to write a happy song. Words and music are included.

Cranberries

William Jaspersohn. Illustrated with photographs by the author. Houghton Mifflin. ISBN 0-395-52098-3. CC '92.

> In this informative account of how cranberries are grown, harvested, and distributed, detailed text of a native American fruit is enhanced by vivid photographs.

Dad's Dinosaur Day

Diane Dawson Hearn. Illustrated by the author. Macmillan. ISBN 0-02-743485-0. CC '94.

When Mikey's father becomes a dinosaur, they share a school day. Dad provides transportation, playground assistance, after-school fun, and a reason to eat and shower outside. Young readers will be amused as they imagine their parents as dinosaurs.

Dear Mr. Blueberry

Simon James. Illustrated by the author. McElderry. ISBN 0-689-50529-9. CC '92.

This is an engaging story of a girl who imagines there is a whale in her pond. She exchanges letters with her teacher, who tries to convince her that a whale could not live in a pond. Through their correspondence we learn facts about whales.

Diane Goode's Book of Silly Stories & Songs

Illustrated by Diane Goode. Dutton. ISBN 0-525-44967-1. CC '92.

These silly stories come from all over the world and have been crafted to blend into this book, which shares folklore and songs along with illustrations that will delight the viewer. Complete with thorough introduction and source notes.

Dinosaurs at the Supermarket

Lindsay Camp. Illustrated by Clare Skilbeck. Viking. ISBN 0-670-84802-6. CC '94.

Laura and her best friend, an imaginary crocodile, discover a dinosaur bone while digging for buried treasure. The next morning a dinosaur and his friends appear. Thinking he wants his bone back, Laura leads him on a merry chase.

Illustration ©1992 by William Steig from his Doctor De Soto Goes to Africa. *Reprinted by permission of Michael di Capua Books/HarperCollins Publishers.*

Dinostory
Michaela Morgan. Illustrated by True Kelley. Dutton. ISBN 0-525-44726-1. CC '92.

> Andrew Gilmore is crazy about dinosaurs. On his birthday, he makes his wish known to a wizard, who makes many dinosaurs appear. Andrew discovers that dinosaurs are not that much fun.

Doctor De Soto Goes to Africa
William Steig. Illustrated by the author. Michael di Capua/HarperCollins. ISBN 0-06-205002-8. CC '92.

> After a cablegram from Mudambo, an elephant with an unbearable toothache, the world-famous dentist Doctor De Soto and his wife travel to Africa. However, before he is able to care for the elephant, De Soto is kidnaped by Honkitonk, an angry evil monkey.

Dogs Don't Wear Sneakers
Laura Numeroff. Illustrated by Joe Mathieu. Simon & Schuster. ISBN 0-671-79525-2. CC '94.

>The author of *If You Give a Mouse a Cookie* has again created a lively rhythmic text containing a menagerie of animal characters involved in very uncharacteristic activities. Humorous comparisons between ourselves and other beasties will give readers a chuckle.

The Dog Who Found Christmas
Linda Jennings. Illustrated by Catherine Walters. Dutton. ISBN 0-525-45155-2. CC '94.

>This poignant Christmas tale addresses the need for responsible pet ownership. The little dog Buster's beautifully illustrated search for a new home and its happy conclusion are presented thoughtfully.

The Dog Who Had Kittens
Polly Robertus. Illustrated by Janet Stevens. Holiday House. ISBN 0-8234-0860-4. CC '92.

>Baxter, the Bassett Hound, lifted his head and howled, thinking, "Just what I need, more cats around the place!" But he soon begins spending all his time with the kittens until one day he discovers their box empty. Stevens's illustrations capture the humor and sentiment in this favorite of 1st graders.

Don't Wake Up Mama! Another Five Little Monkeys Story
Eileen Christelow. Illustrated by the author. Clarion. ISBN 0-395-60176-2. CC '92.

>Those five little monkeys are back! This time, it's Mama's birthday, and they bake her a cake and make her a present. CRASH! BANG! THUD! Can they do it without waking Mama? Hilarious antics made this a favorite of younger readers.

Dragon's Fat Cat
Dave Pilkey. Illustrated by the author. Orchard. ISBN 0-531-05982-0. CC '92.

> Through humorous trial and error, Dragon learns what is involved in cat care. Children especially enjoy Dragon's interpretation of a "litter box" and the surprising five-kitten ending.

Earthquake in the Third Grade
Laurie Myers. Illustrated by Karen Ritz. Clarion. ISBN 0-395-65360-6. CC '94.

> Using an ant farm earthquake as an example in this warm and entertaining story, the author draws a parallel as to how both ants and people must challenge themselves to make the best of unexpected circumstances.

The Easter Egg Farm
Mary Jane Auch. Illustrated by the author. Holiday House. ISBN 0-8234-0917-1. CC '92.

> The theme of individuality is woven through the delightful spring story of Pauline the hen who lays the most colorful and unusual eggs. Although Pauline's owner, Mrs. Pennywort, enthusiastically encourages Pauline's creativity, Pauline's peers do not. Several second graders commented that they hoped the other hens would learn to accept Pauline's uniqueness.

Elvira
Margaret Shannon. Illustrated by the author. Ticknor & Fields. ISBN 0-395-66597-3. CC '94.

> Children love dragon stories, and this is no exception. Elvira is a young dragon from a fire-breathing, princess-devouring family who would rather act like a princess than a dragon! Young readers delight in how Elvira changes the other dragons' perspective. First published in Australia by Omnibus Books.

Ezra in Pursuit: The Great Maze Chase

Rosalyn Schanzer. Illustrated by the author. Doubleday/ Bantam Doubleday Dell. ISBN 0-385-30884-1. CC '94.

> A boy in pajamas and cowboy attire chases outlaws through the Old West and Central and South America. Bright, colorful, detailed pages contain mazes, humor, rhyming words, and facts about 1874. Please notice the page opposite the title page!

For Laughing Out Loud: Poems to Tickle Your Funnybone

Selected by Jack Prelutsky. Illustrated by Marjorie Priceman. Knopf. ISBN 0-394-82144-0. CC '92.

> Just as the title suggests, Prelutsky has collected a book of poems to "tickle your funny bone." The book contains humorous poems by an array of American writers and includes author and title indexes.

Fritz and the Mess Fairy

Rosemary Wells. Illustrated by the author. Dial. ISBN 0-8037-0981-1. CC '92.

> Not only was Fritz so messy that he couldn't find things in his own room, he created difficulties for his sisters and parents. After a visit from the "mess fairy," who was even sloppier than Fritz, he decided to change his ways—almost.

Frog Medicine

Mark Teague. Illustrated by the author. Scholastic. ISBN 0-590-44177-9. CC '92.

> A boy named Elmo finds himself stuck doing a report on a book called *Frog Medicine*. Worse, he begins turning into a frog. By traveling to Frogtown, he learns valuable lessons about frogs, homework, and life. Some second graders surmised that, "If you don't do your work, you'll get the big 'F', Frog Legs!"

George Washington's Mother

Jean Fritz. Illustrated by DyAnne DiSalvo-Ryan. Putnam & Grosset. ISBN 448-40385-4. CC '92.

> The life and times of Mary Ball Washington, her famous son George, and her other children are described in an easy flowing narrative with numerous well-drawn color illustrations.

Go Away, Big Green Monster!

Ed Emberley. Illustrated by the author. Little, Brown. ISBN 0-316-23653-5. CC '94.

> Die-cut pages create the monster as the reader turns each page, then the process is reversed. The reader commands away each scary feature. The last page instructs "Don't come back," but children will savor the book again and again.

Goldilocks and the Three Bears
Retold by Jonathan Langley. Illustrated by Jonathan Langley.
HarperCollins. ISBN 0-06-020814-7. CC '94.

> Although this retelling follows the familiar pattern of the
> classic fairy tale, the story's hint of further adventures for
> Goldilocks, such as slaying dragons, appeals to young
> listeners.

Granny Greenteeth and the Noise in the Night
Kenn and Joanne Compton. Illustrated by Kenn Compton.
Holiday House. ISBN 0-8234-1051-X. CC '94.

> Children will enjoy sharing this delightful, cumulative ver-
> sion of a traditional tale. The repetitive elements, along with
> humorous illustrations, make this book a favorite.

Green Wilma
Tedd Arnold. Illustrated by the author. Dial. ISBN 0-8037-
1313-4. CC '94.

> Wilma has turned green overnight, setting the stage for a
> humorous day as she finds out it's not easy being green.

The Grumpalump
Sarah Hayes. Illustrated by Barbara Firth. Clarion. ISBN 0-
89919-871-6. CC '92.

> In the tradition of "The House That Jack Built," rhythm and
> rhyme combine with a surprise ending to delight young read-
> ers. Just what is a grumpalump? The guessing game can con-
> tinue page by page.

Hector's New Sneakers
Amanda Vesey. Illustrated by the author. Viking. ISBN 0-670-
84882-4. CC '94.

> All Hector wanted for his birthday were the sneakers every-
> one else had, but he receives a slightly different pair. This
> delightful story shows that being different can be a winning
> situation!

Henry's Wild Morning

Margaret Greaves. Illustrated by Teresa O'Brien. Dial. ISBN 0-8037-0907-2. CC '92.

> Henry is the runt of the litter and the only striped kitten, but he imagines he is a fierce tiger and has a wild and mischievous adventure. Bold and colorful illustrations made this a favorite of 1st and 2nd graders.

The Holiday Handwriting School

Robin Pulver. Illustrated by G. Brian Karas. Four Winds. ISBN 0-02-775455-3. CC '92.

> Santa, Tooth Fairy, and Easter Bunny experience difficulty with their handwriting. Mrs. Holiday offers personal advice and in return receives loving mementos from her special students. One reader commented, "Mrs. Holiday was nice because she helped them to write." Others enjoyed "the happy ending."

How Giraffe Got Such a Long Neck...And Why Rhino Is So Grumpy

Retold by Michael Rosen. Illustrated by John Clementson. Dial. ISBN 0-8037-1621-4. CC '94.

> Children always wanting to know "why" gleefully respond to how the giraffe got such a long neck and why the rhino is so grumpy in this retelling of an old African folk tale. First published in Great Britain by Studio Edition as *The First Giraffe*.

If You Give a Moose a Muffin

Laura Joffe Numeroff. Illustrated by Felicia Bond. Harper Collins. ISBN 0-06-024405-4. CC '92.

> This circular tale is a comic sequel to *If You Give a Mouse a Cookie*. The much larger moose creates some hilarious situations when he visits a young boy and eats all the muffins.

Inside the Whale and Other Animals

Illustrated by Ted Dewan. Text by Steve Parker. Bantam Doubleday Dell. ISBN 0-385-30651-2. CC '92.

> Easy-to-follow diagrams and colorful pictures introduce children to the world inside whales and other animals. The detailed illustrations provide large visual information for young readers.

Jeremy's Tail

Duncan Ball. Illustrated by Donna Rawlins. Orchard. ISBN 0-531-05951-0. CC '92.

> Jeremy entertains readers as he travels around the world trying to pin the tail on a donkey that was in his own house. The illustrations show various parts of the world and stress determination.

Jingle the Christmas Clown

Tomie dePaola. Illustrated by the author. Putnam. ISBN 0-399-22338-X. CC '92.

> "Only we 'vecchietti'—old-timers—are left," explains the barber to the circus troupe. "So we won't be celebrating Christmas here this year," the mayor adds. "And we certainly can't afford the circus either." Tomie dePaola's rich, colorful paintings capture the spirit of Christmas as a young clown and his baby animals bring cheer to the poor Italian villagers.

A Job for Wittilda

Caralyn Buehner. Illustrated by Mark Buehner. Dial. ISBN 0-8037-1149-2. CC '94.

> The job market is tough to crack for witches like Wittilda, but she must earn a living to care for all her cats. While listeners appreciated the humor in Wittilda's various vocations, the numerous cat illustrations generated the most kudos.

John F. Kennedy: Young People's President
Catherine Corley Anderson. Illustrated with photographs.
Lerner. ISBN 0-8225-4904-2. CC '92.

> This book describes the life and times of President John
> Fitzgerald Kennedy, who grew up in a large Irish family in
> Boston, Massachusetts. Children can relate to the manner in
> which this story is told.

King of the Playground
Phyllis Reynolds Naylor. Illustrated by Nola Langner Malone.
Atheneum. ISBN 0-689-31558-9. CC '92.

> Kevin is afraid of Sammy, who has declared himself "King of
> the Playground." After several talks with his father, Kevin
> has the courage to confront the bully. The story lends itself to
> discussions of courage and problem solving.

Make a Splash! Care About the Ocean
Thompson Yardley. Illustrated by the author. Millbrook. ISBN
1-56294-147-X. CC '92.

> "It had informative facts and tiny comiclike pictures," wrote
> one third grader about this introduction to the ocean focus-
> ing on industrial, recreational, and environmental issues.
> Bold captions, a short lively text in easy-to-read/browse for-
> mat, and watercolor sketches offer a wealth of information
> appropriate for second through fourth graders.

Max's Dragon Shirt
Rosemary Wells. Illustrated by the author. Dial. ISBN 0-8037-
0944-7. CC '92.

> Follow Max and Ruby as they shop in a department store.
> Max's determination to get a dragon shirt leads him away
> from his distracted sister and into trouble in this hilarious
> read-aloud romp.

Mona the Brilliant

Sonia Holleyman. Illustrated by the author. Doubleday/ Bantam Doubleday Dell. ISBN 0-385-30907-4. CC '94.

> Mona is brilliant, and so are her ideas for earning money to replace her old bike. A hair stylist she's not, but she tries it for the money. Will she raise enough?

Mona the Vampire

Sonia Holleyman. Illustrated by the author. Delacorte. ISBN 0-385-30286-X. CC '92.

> The outlandish antics of Mona and her cat Fang disrupt school and ballet class as she pretends to be a vampire. Mona keeps the reader eager to see what she will do next.

The Moon Clock

Matt Faulkner. Illustrated by the author. Scholastic. ISBN 0-590-41593-X. CC '92.

> In this fantasy, a little girl stays home from school because the other children tease her. A captain from a different place enters her room through her toy chest and cheers her on to brave deeds. The illustrations are wonderful!

Mrs. Katz and Tush

Patricia Polacco. Illustrated by the author. Bantam Doubleday Dell. ISBN 0-553-08122-5. CC '92.

> Knowing that Mrs. Katz is a widow, Larnel asks her to adopt a kitten. As they care for the kitten together, Larnel realizes that her Jewish heritage and his Black history create a special bond between them.

Mrs. Wolf

Shen Roddie. Illustrated by Korky Paul. Dial. ISBN 0-8037-1300-2. CC '94.

> When Lambert falls into Mrs. Wolf's den, she asks him to stay for dinner. But will Lambert be the main course? Clever pop-ups add appeal, prompting one child to write: "The fun pictures are the best part."

From Mucky Moose *by Jonathan Allen. Illustration ©1991 by Jonathan Allen. Reprinted by permission of the Simon & Schuster Children's Publishing Division.*

Mucky Moose

Jonathan Allen. Illustrated by the author. Macmillan. ISBN 0-02-700251-9. CC '92.

> Mucky, the muckiest, smelliest moose that ever lived, is pursued by the biggest wolf in the forest and he's extra hungry? Humorous illustrations depict the wolf's attempt to eat Mucky and the unexpected outcome.

My Great-Aunt Arizona

Gloria Houston. Illustrated by Susan Condie Lamb. HarperCollins. ISBN 0-06-022602-4. CC '93.

> Arizona loved to read, and that began her life of teaching and the love of learning she brought to generations of students in the Blue Ridge Mountains. Clear words and beautiful illustrations tell the story of the author's real great-aunt—inspiring!

My Mother the Cat
Katherine Potter. Illustrated by the author. Simon & Schuster. ISBN 0-671-79632-1. CC '94.

> Sent to bed for feeding her dinner to the cat, Jane makes a wish and discovers the next morning that it has come true. Her mother is curled up fast asleep in a basket, purring. Puff, the cat, lets Jane do anything she wants.

No Milk!
Jennifer A. Ericsson. Illustrated by Ora Eitan. Tambourine. ISBN 0-688-11306-0. CC '94.

> An "udderly appealing story" of a city boy who tries to coax milk from a dairy cow. He juggles, tells jokes, sings, and dances—but no milk! Finally, he discovers the success of a pat, a squeeze, and a little tug.

No Plain Pets!
Marc Ian Barasch. Illustrated by Henrik Drescher. Harper-Collins. ISBN 0-06-022472-X. CC '92.

> Will an ordinary pet cat, dog, or pony do? A young boy's search for the right pet is vividly displayed in color and rhyme as he soars and sails using his imagination.

Now Everybody Really Hates Me
Jane Read Martin and Patricia Marx. Illustrated by Roz Chast. HarperCollins. ISBN 0-06-021293-4. CC '94.

> All children can identify with sibling revenge and being sent to their room! Pouty Patty Jane Pepper echoes their sentiments. After all, she didn't hit her brother Theodore, she only touched him hard! Kids will ask for this one again and again!

One Hundred Hungry Ants

Elinor J. Pinczes. Illustrated by Bonnie MacKain. Houghton Mifflin. ISBN 0-395-63116-5. CC '94.

> "Hi dee ho!" 100 orderly ants head for a picnic in single file. To go faster, they try two lines of 50, and then 4 lines of 25, and so on. But with all that regrouping, they miss lunch!

The Paper Bag Prince

Colin Thompson. Illustrated by the author. Knopf. ISBN 0-679-83048-0. CC '92.

> Colorful, detailed illustrations captivate young readers as the Paper Bag Prince moves into the town dump. Living in an abandoned train, he observes nature slowly reclaiming the polluted earth.

Peeping Beauty

Mary Jane Auch. Illustrated by the author. Holiday House. ISBN 0-8234-1001-3. CC '94.

> Does the fox really want to hire the hen to dance in the new ballet called Peeping Beauty or does he plan to make her his next meal? Children enjoyed finding the answer in this colorfully illustrated book.

Pets of the Presidents

Janet Caulkins. Illustrated with photographs. Millbrook. ISBN 1-56294-060-0. CC '92.

> Besides the usual dogs and cats, U.S. presidents have had many different kinds of pets. President Lincoln had a goat, and Theodore Roosevelt had snakes! As you read about the pets, you get to see a different side of the presidents and learn a little about life in the White House.

Pigs Aplenty, Pigs Galore!

David McPhail. Illustrated by the author. Dutton. ISBN 0-525-45079-3. CC '94.

> Pigs of all shapes and sizes (even an Elvis porker) cavort around a nonplused man, quietly reading in his easy chair.

Although he finally stops the antics, readers know all is forgiven when he falls asleep dreaming of more pigs.

Polar Bear, Polar Bear, What Do You Hear?
Bill Martin Jr. Illustrated by Eric Carle. Holt. ISBN 0-8050-1759-3. CC '92.

> Do you know the sounds that the 200 animals make? The animals hear each other growling, snorting, and hissing, and zoo keeper hears the children imitating the animals. This is a wonderful chant-along book.

Pudmuddles
Carol Beach York. Illustrated by Lisa Thiesing. HarperCollins. ISBN 0-06-020436-2. CC '94.

> This is an imaginative and humorous story about Mr. Pudmuddle, who likes to do everything in a backward way. When he marries Mrs. Pudmuddle, he finds he will have to change some of his ways and she will have to compromise as well...eating dinner in the morning?

Illustration from Polar Bear, Polar Bear, What Do You Hear? *by Bill Martin, Jr. Illustrations ©1991 by Eric Carle. Reprinted by permission of Henry Holt and Company.*

The Rainbow Fish

Marcus Pfister. Translated by J. Alison James. Illustrated by the author. North-South Books. ISBN 1-55858-009-3. CC '92.

> Children love the eye-catching, glittering scales that illustrate the rainbow fish, who is very proud of his beauty but soon learns that his beauty alone does not bring him happiness.

Rats on the Range and Other Stories

James Marshall. Illustrated by the author. Dial. ISBN 0-8037-1384-3. CC '94.

> In eight short stories by James Marshall, animals show a wide range of human foibles. From Miss Mouse, who keeps house for a tomcat, to Buzzard Watkins, who outwits his heirs, try to pick your favorite.

Rosie's Baby Tooth

Maryann Macdonald. Illustrated by Melissa Sweet. Atheneum. ISBN 0-689-31626-7. CC '92.

> Rosie isn't sure she likes losing a baby tooth and then giving it to the Tooth Fairy, so she writes to the Tooth Fairy. The letter she receives convinces Rosie that losing baby teeth can be special after all.

Ruby the Copycat

Peggy Rathmann. Illustrated by the author. Scholastic. ISBN 0-590-43747-X. CC '92.

> This is a charming, humorous, sensitive tale about self-identification. Everywhere children are searching for acceptance and approval. With the help of Miss Hart, her teacher, Ruby realizes her own worth.

Rumpelstiltskin

Retold by Jonathan Langley. Illustrated by the author. HarperCollins. ISBN 0-06-020198-3. CC '92.

> This lighthearted retelling of *Rumpelstiltskin* will delight children of all ages. The subtle humor, in both words and

illustrations, will hold interest while remaining faithful to the well-known tale.

Sam's Surprise
David Pilham. Illustrated by the author. Dutton. ISBN 0-525-44947-7. CC '92.

> A humorous sequel to *Sam's Sandwich*, the rhyming verse tells of Sam's birthday party. In a sister's revenge, Samantha has treats for all his friends. Oh, what surprises she has for them! Wonderful and funny.

From Seven Little Hippos *by Mike Thaler. Illustration ©1991 by Jerry Smath. Reprinted by permission of the publisher, Half Moon Books, a division of Simon & Schuster.*

Sea Squares

Joy N. Hulme. Illustrated by Carol Schwartz. Hyperion. ISBN 1-56282-079-6. CC '92.

> Counting and multiplication facts are discovered with playful rhymes featuring ocean creatures such as "four slippery seals, with four flippers each...[making] 16 flippery feet." The pictures and border designs complete the watery scene.

Seven Little Hippos

Mike Thaler. Illustrated by Jerry Smath. Simon & Schuster. ISBN 0-671-72964-0. CC '92.

> In this delightful predictable book, children recognize the similarity to the familiar "Five Little Monkeys" rhyme. Chil-

dren of all ages will be thrilled by the surprise ending after the doctor leaves.

Siegfried
Diane Stanley. Illustrated by John Sandford. Bantam. ISBN 0-553-07022-3. CC '92.

> Cat lovers will feel at home with Siegfried, a very old cat who has difficulty adapting to the sound of the cuckoo clock that enters his home one Christmas. The illustrations are warm and inviting and set the mood.

Silly Sally
Audrey Wood. Illustrated by the author. Harcourt Brace & Company. ISBN 0-15-274428-2. CC '92.

> A catchy, rhyming cumulative tale of the unusual procession of Silly Sally and the friends she meets while traveling to town—dancing backwards and upside down.

Illustration from Siegfried *by Diane Stanley. Illustrations ©1991 by John Sandford. Reprinted by permission of Bantam Little Rooster.*

Slombo the Gross

Rodney A. Greenblat. Illustrated by the author. Harper-Collins. ISBN 0-06-020775-2. CC '94.

> Even though Slombo is gross and lives by the dump, the creatures all love him. When he saves the day by helping the town, the skunks, and the Swamp Beast, Slombo is a hero!

Smart Dog

Ralph Leemis. Illustrated by Chris L. Demarest. Boyds Mills Press. ISBN 1-56397-109-7. CC '94.

> Kids delight in stretching their imaginations with "what ifs," but what would really happen if they owned a smart dog? Would their dreams of fame, fortune, and happiness come true?

Some Birthday!

Patricia Polacco. Illustrated by the author. Simon & Schuster. ISBN 0-671-72750-8. CC '92.

> Patricia is concerned that her father forgot her birthday. This well written and illustrated story describes the scariest and most exciting birthday anyone could have.

Song Lee in Room 2B

Suzy Kline. Illustrated by Frank Remkiewicz. Viking. ISBN 0-670-84772-0. CC '94.

> Room 2B is a typical classroom, with Harry and his antics, Doug and his talking, Mary and her nosiness, and many other students we all recognize. Quiet, shy Song Lee, however, surprises classmates and readers with her creativity and courage.

The Sub

P.J. Petersen. Illustrated by Meredith Johnson. Dutton. ISBN 0-525-45059-9. CC '94.

> Two boys switch their identities when a substitute teacher comes to their class. The joke backfires, and both boys end up wishing they had never perpetrated the hoax.

Take Time to Relax!
Nancy Carlson. Illustrated by the author. Viking. ISBN 0-670-83287-1. CC '92.

> What does a busy family do when they become snowbound? Tina, her mom, and her dad are always rushing from one activity to another. They learn that being home can also be fun.

That's Good! That's Bad!
Margery Cuyler. Illustrated by David Catrow. Holt. ISBN 0-8050-1535-3. CC '92.

> Children learn to expect the unexpected in this vividly illustrated tale. A little boy's adventures (That's good!) and misadventures (That's bad!) with his jungle friends are told in an appealing, repetitive pattern that children love.

Illustration from That's Good! That's Bad! *by Margery Cuyler. Illustrations ©1991 by David Catrow. Reprinted by permission of Henry Holt and Company.*

Three Billy Goats Gruff
Retold by Glen Rounds. Illustrated by Glen Rounds. Holiday House. ISBN 0-8234-1015-3. Holiday House. CC '94.

> Bold, heavy type encourages listeners to join in the reading of this familiar tale. The big, ugly troll prompted one youngster to comment, "He's the best part."

The Three-Legged Cat
Margaret Mahy. Illustrated by Jonathan Allen. Viking. ISBN 0-670-85015-2. CC '94.

> Young readers will enjoy being privy to the plot twist of this humorous tale. A ragamuffin cat escapes from a life of boredom by posing as a toupee. Text descriptions are a perfect match with the bright illustrations.

The Three Little Wolves and the Big Bad Pig
Eugene Trivizas. Illustrated by Helen Oxenbury. Margaret K. McElderry Books. ISBN 0-689-50569-8. CC '94.

> What kind of house do three little wolves have to build to be safe from the big bad pig? Young readers delighted in this altered retelling of the traditional conflict between wolf and pig. Be prepared for a surprise ending!

Tiger, Tiger, Growing Up
Joan Hewett. Illustrated with photographs by Richard Hewett. Clarion. ISBN 0-395-61583-6. CC '94.

> The photographs especially appealed to students, who were fascinated with the efforts of the staff at Sea World Africa who raised an infant tiger.

Today Is Monday
Retold by Eric Carle. Illustrated by Eric Carle. Philomel. ISBN 0-399-21966-8. CC '94.

> Today is Monday will be enjoyed by children because of the repetitive text and delightful illustrations of the popular children's song. A wonderful way to reinforce the days of the week with young readers.

Tomorrow on Rocky Pond

Lynn Reiser. Illustrated by the author. Greenwillow. ISBN 0-688-10672-2. CC '94.

> This adventure will delight the reader with its vivid pictures and in-depth descriptions of all that is happening at Rocky Pond!

Trouble with Trolls

Jan Brett. Illustrated by the author. Putnam. ISBN 399-22336-3. CC '92.

> A real conflict develops between the trolls, who very much desire a dog, and Treva, the feisty heroine, who outwits one troll after another. As usual, Jan Brett has filled this story with eye-catching detail.

Two Badd Babies

Jeffie Ross Gordon. Illustrated by Chris L. Demarest. Boyds Mills Press. ISBN 1-878093-85-1. CC '92.

> Children loved the adventures of the "Badd" babies, who bounce and rock their playpen to the baker, movies, hamburger stand, their dad's bookstore, and home again. "I couldn't stop laughing!" exclaimed one second grader. "It was so funny that it must have been a dream." The comical illustrations match the text to create a hilarious and exciting story.

Walt Disney's Mickey and the Beanstalk

Retold by Teddy Slater. Illustrated by Phil Wilson. Disney Press. ISBN 1-56282-385-X. CC '94.

> This adaptation of Jack and the Beanstalk will delight elementary readers. They will enjoy the vivid illustrations from the Disney movie, and finding Mickey Mouse and Goofy with their friends will add to their pleasure.

Illustration from Trouble with Trolls *by Jan Brett. ©1992 by Jan Brett. Reprinted by permission of G.P. Putnam's Sons.*

Water

François Michel. Paper engineering by François Michel. Illustrated by Yves Larvor. Lothrop, Lee & Shepard. ISBN 0-688-11427-X. CC '94.

> "Water is the source of all life." So begins Michel in his educational picture book about the most precious substance on earth. Large realistic illustrations and lift-the-flap picture format delight younger readers. Middle grade readers will enjoy the broad scope of information in this valuable resource. First published in France as Le Livre Animé de L'eau by Bayard Éditions.

Way Out West Lives a Coyote Named Frank

Jillian Lund. Illustrated by the author. Dutton. ISBN 0-525-44982-5. CC '94.

> Against a whimsical, yet authentic background of the American Southwest, Frank has a busy but satisfying life. The simple text explains "what coyotes do best way out West."

Whales: A First Discovery Book

Created by Gallimard Jeunesse, Claude Delafosse, Ute Fuhr, and Raoul Sautai. Illustrated by Ute Fuhr and Raoul Sautai. Scholastic. ISBN 0-590-47130-9. CC '94.

> Whales are amazing animals! A concise explanation of these gigantic mammals is accompanied by annotated illustrations and colorful overlays. This was a favorite of first and second graders. Originally published in France in 1991 by Editions Gallimard.

Where's That Bus?

Eileen Browne. Illustrated by the author. Simon & Schuster. ISBN 0-671-73810-0. CC '92.

> Two friends, Rabbit and Mole, try to catch a bus to visit Squirrel. While waiting for the bus, Rabbit and Mole get distracted and don't see the buses that pass by. Where's that bus? Just wait and see!

From Who Are You? *by John Schindell. Illustrations* ©1991 *by James Watts. Courtesy Margaret K. McElderry Books, an imprint of Simon & Schuster Children's Publishing Division.*

Who Are You?

John Schindel. Illustrated by James Watts. McElderry. ISBN 0-689-50523-X. CC '92.

> "You are too little, too small, too young..." are unwelcome words to children's ears. Brown Bear's parents wisely allow him to discover for himself that it is much more fun to be Brown Bear than to be a grownup.

The Widow's Broom

Chris Van Allsburg. Illustrated by the author. Houghton Mifflin. ISBN 0-395-64051-2. CC '92.

> Veiled in mystery in text and illustration, Van Allsburg's newest offering portrays strange happenings in the life of village neighbors. Widow Minna Shaw teaches a witch's broom new tricks. Her neighbors want to destroy the evil broom. Multileveled meanings enhance the value of this treasure.

Yo, Hungry Wolf!

David Vozar. Illustrated by Betsy Lewin. Pitspopany Press, formerly Doubleday/Bantam Doubleday Dell. ISBN 0-385-30452-8. CC '94.

> Favorite fairy tales in contemporary, upbeat, way-in rap. If you cannot read in rap, the text and illustrations will carry you through; then youngsters will smile and beg you to read it again.

Middle Grades

The A-to-Z Book of Cars
Angela Royston. Illustrated by Terry Pastor. Barron's. ISBN 0-8120-6209-4. CC '92.

> "Mint!" That's what a group of 6th graders said after reading this book. This illustrated alphabet book of cars starts with Alfa Romeo and ends with the Zodiac Zephyr. A must read for all car buffs!

Alice in April
Phyllis Reynolds Naylor. Atheneum. ISBN 0-689-31805-7. CC '94.

> April Fool's Day, her 13th birthday, being woman of the house, and getting named by the 7th grade boys are some of the reasons why April is so difficult for Alice. Middle readers will surely laugh and cry with her as she confronts the difficulties of growing up.

Alligators to Zooplankton: A Dictionary of Water Babies
Les Kaufman and the Staff of the New England Aquarium. Illustrated with photographs. Franklin Watts. ISBN 0-531-15215-4. CC '92.

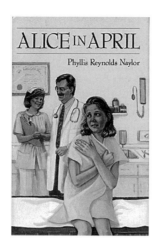

This A to Z book about aquatic animals and their young offers fascinating information and photographs. Many unusual stories are told about different ways that life begins in the water.

American Tall Tales

Mary Pope Osborne. Illustrated with wood engravings by Michael McCurdy. Knopf. ISBN 0-679-80089-1. CC '92.

> Stories of America's first folk heroes, including Davy Crockett, Paul Bunyan, Sally Ann Thunder, Ann Whirlwind, and 6 other unique characters, are sure to make you laugh. Historical notes give background about each character.

The Baby-Sitters Club Chain Letter

Ann M. Martin. Scholastic. ISBN 0-590-47151-1. CC '94.

> Club members overcome the summer doldrums by starting a chain letter that has interesting rules. Realistic letters and postcards, some placed in envelopes, would be great for letter-writing units!

The Battle of Lexington and Concord
Neil Johnson. Illustrated with full-color photographs by the author. Four Winds Press. ISBN 0-02-747841-6. CC '92.

> A clear, detailed text and color photographs taken in Boston, Lexington, and Concord bring to life this account of "The shot heard round the world." Readable narrative style and action photos draw the reader into this account of the events of April 19, 1775, and its implications.

Best Enemies Again
Kathleen Leverich. Illustrated by Walter Lorraine. Greenwillow. ISBN 0-688-09440-6. CC '92.

> Felicity Doll is back, this time to challenge Priscilla in the lemonade business. And when poor speller Priscilla gets a "study buddy" to help her, it's none other than Felicity, the snake? The rivalry continues in this humorous, easy chapter book.

Best Friends
Elisabeth Reuter. Illustrated by Antoinette Becker. Yellow Brick Road Press. ISBN 0-943706-18-1. CC '94.

> Judith and Lisa were best friends until Hitler began persuading the German people that all their problems were due to the Jews. This emotional and thoughtful story shows what happens to friendship when people are forced to change their beliefs. First published in German under the title *Judith and Lisa*, copyright 1988 Verlag Heinrich Ellermann, Munich.

Bingo
Adapted by Beth Goodman. Illustrated with photographs. Scholastic. ISBN 0-590-45039-5. CC '92.

> Children are enchanted with Bingo, an amazing and helpful dog. After leaving he circus, he rescues Chuckie from a burning building, helps capture robbers, and meets other challenges. "Bingo is a real hero," said a 4th grader. "I wish he were my dog."

The Boy Who Sailed with Columbus

Michael Foreman. Illustrated by the author. Arcade. ISBN 1-55970-178-1. CC '92.

> The perilous journey with Columbus and life in the New World are told from the viewpoint of Leif, a young orphan. His growth from boy to man, from European to simple native, is powerful and thought-provoking.

The Children's Space Atlas

Robin Kerrod. Millbrook. ISBN 1-56294-100-3. CC '92.

> Children enjoy poring over the pages of this large book loaded with colorful photographs and drawings. Statistics and interesting facts and history about our solar system, stars, and space exploration abound.

Coyote Steals the Blanket: A Ute Tale

Retold by Janet Stevens. Illustrated by Janet Stevens. Holiday House. ISBN 0-8234-0996-1. CC '94.

> Coyote brags, bosses, and shows off. When he steals a blanket, a rock chases him. He doesn't listen or give up. He runs away from the consequences of his actions. Coyote loses his friends but still doesn't learn his lesson.

Custer

Deborah King. Illustrated by the author. Philomel. ISBN 0-399-22147-6. CC '92.

> Custer wants no fame or greatness. He just wants to be a horse, although at times he thinks he's a cow. Then he meets Minto, a wild gray mare, and his life changes forever. A love story for horse lovers.

David Robinson: NBA Super Center

Bill Gutman. Illustrated with photographs. Millbrook. ISBN 1-56294-228-X. CC '94.

> This biography of the African American basketball star gives brief information on his happy childhood as a gifted student and his adult personal life, but the book focuses mainly on his basketball playing at the U.S. Naval Academy and as a NBA star.

Die for Me

Carol Gorman. Avon. ISBN 0-380-76686-8. CC '92.

> Holly Baldwin is dead, and the only clue is the Ouija board's message that more will die. Even the suspects are frightened. This story is scary enough to keep young readers turning pages until the surprising conclusion.

Discovering Christopher Columbus: How History Is Invented

Kathy Pelta. Illustrated with photographs. Lerner. ISBN 0-8225-4899-2. CC '92.

> This book not only explores the story of Christopher Columbus but also delves into the research process. It takes a historical look at information to try to determine fact.

Dogteam

Gary Paulsen. Illustrated by Ruth Wright Paulsen. Delacorte/Bantam Doubleday Dell. ISBN 0-385-30550-8. CC '94.

> It is midnight on a cold, moonlit night. A musher takes a team of dogs on their nocturnal run, and the magic of that special moment appeals even to readers unfamiliar with the ritual and far removed from northern climates.

Don't Read This Book, Whatever You Do! More Poems About School

Kalli Dakos. Illustrated by G. Brian Karas. Four Winds. ISBN 0-02-725582-4. CC '94.

> Humorous poems and minidialogues about great and not-so-great moments in elementary school. Students will be able to identify with the moments of triumph, failure, embarrassment, and frustration. Adults will recognize many students in their lives.

The Earth and Sky

Jean-Pierre Verdet. Illustrated by Sylvaine Perols. Cartwheel Books/Scholastic. ISBN 0-590-45268-1. CC '92.

> Colorful back-to-front overlays show such aspects as the earth's core and underground rivers. Moon phases and planets appearing in the night sky are shown in glossy, color illustrations. A valuable resource certain to attract young readers.

Earthquake

Christopher Lampton. Millbrook. ISBN 1-56294-031-7. CC '92.

> General information about earthquakes and specific attention to the San Francisco earthquakes of 1906 and 1989 provide descriptions about the dangers of earthquakes. One class of 4th graders agreed the pictures were colorful, real, and showed action.

Fourth Grade Rats

Jerry Spinelli. Illustrated by Paul Casale. Scholastic. ISBN 0-590-44243-0, CC '92.

> "I wouldn't want to turn into a rat!" wrote one 4th grader. This is an appealing story for intermediate students about growing up and peer pressure. "A funny book that's easy to read," said another 4th grader.

George Washington: The Man Who Would Not Be King
Stephen Krensky. Illustrated from various sources. Scholastic. ISBN 0-590-43730-5. CC '92.

> Imagine this change in history: King George of America! This book is the story of a man popular enough to have been chosen king but wise enough to refuse.

The Ghost of Popcorn Hill
Betty Ren Wright. Illustrated by Karen Ritz. Holiday House. ISBN 0-8234-1009-9. CC '94.

> "Unpredictable" and "adventuresome" were two typical descriptors praising this story of two boys uniting a dual set of ghosts: a lonesome old man and a dog looking for a companion.

The Giant Book of the Mummy
Rosalie David. Illustrated by Nick Harris and Roger Stewart. Lodestar. ISBN 0-525-67413-6. CC '94.

> Tutankhamen's treasures provide the detail for six two-page spreads and one single page on the back cover outlining the young pharaoh's reign, burial, and tomb discovery. Readers describe this big book as "awesome," "gross," and "full of information and pictures."

Go Hang a Salami! I'm a Lasagna Hog! and Other Palindromes
Jon Agee. Illustrated by the author. Farrar, Straus & Giroux. ISBN 0-374-33473-0. CC '92.

> This laugh-out-loud book of palindromes—words and phrases spelled the same forward or backward—is illustrated with humorous cartoons. "Hah! Hah! Going in reverse is funny. Loved 'Did mom pop? Mom did,' " wrote a young reader.

Goodbye, Vietnam

Gloria Whelan. Knopf. ISBN 0-679-82263-1. CC '92.

> Fleeing their beloved Vietnam village to seek freedom from a cruel government, Mai and her family face dangers on sea and uncertainties in a Hong Kong refugee camp that readers found "exciting, sad, even funny at times, and very adventurous."

How on Earth Do We Recycle Paper?

Helen Jill Fletcher (crafts) and Seli Groves (text). Illustrated by Art Seiden. Millbrook. ISBN 1-56294-140-2. CC '92.

> Using pictures, diagrams, and easily understandable text, this book describes how paper is produced and recycled. Excellent, creative craft projects using paper or cardboard discards are included at the back of the book.

How to Be Cool in the Third Grade

Betsy Duffey. Illustrated by Janet Wilson. Viking. ISBN 0-670-84798-4. CC '94.

> In this enjoyable chapter book, Robbie York is in the third grade and wonders what it is to be cool. He discovers that answer and how to survive the third-grade bully.

Insect Attack

Christopher Lampton. Illustrated with photographs and diagrams. Millbrook. ISBN 1-56294-127-5. CC '92.

> This thrilling, picture-loaded book details historical accounts of insects that caused disease and crop destruction for centuries. Discusses the life cycles of locusts, mosquitoes, killer bees, and fruit flies, their current threat to humanity, and prevention of future disasters.

Inside Story: The Latest News About Your Body

Mike Lambourne. Millbrook. ISBN 1-56294-148-8. CC '92.

> An overview of the systems of the body. The book is written in a newsy style, full of cartoon-style illustrations. The comments range from "humorous" to "gross." There is a good reading list at the end of the book. Caution: children should not try the experiment on page 8.

Inventions: Inventors & Ingenious Ideas

Peter Turvey. Illustrated by Mark Bergin, Bill Donohoe, Nick Hewetson, John James, Tony Townsend, Hans Wilborg-Jenssen, and Gerald Wood. Franklin Watts. ISBN 0-531-15243-X. CC '92.

> From catapults and magnificent inventions like the steam engine, rocket locomotive, telegraph, airplane, submarine, penicillin, liquid fuel rocket, Model T car, computer, and transistor to futuristic inventions like virtual reality arcade games, these dramatic illustrations "wow" the reader with man's creativity and genius.

Jesse Owens: Olympic Star

Patricia and Fredrick McKissack. Illustrated with photographs; cover illustrated by Ned O.; interior illustrated by Michael David Biegel. Enslow Publishers. ISBN 0-89490-312-8. CC '92.

> Born a sharecropper's son, J.C. Owens grew up as a sickly child and youth. Through perseverance he blossomed into an Olympic jumping and running star, challenging Hitler's dream of German superiority. A heartwarming story of love, sacrifice, and perseverance.

The Kite That Braved Old Orchard Beach

X.J. Kennedy. Illustrated by Marian Young. McElderry. ISBN 0-689-50507-8. CC '92.

> This book captures the thoughts of children in poems that span the years of growing up and the special days in each year. Two great lines are, "With things that matter to me,/not for sale at any price."

The Last Princess: The Story of Princess Ka'iulani of Hawai'i.

Fay Stanley. Illustrated by Diane Stanley. Four Winds. ISBN 0-02-786785-4. CC '92.

> Young readers will admire Princess Ka'iulani, the last heir of the Hawaiian throne, who fought bravely to preserve the rights of her people during a time of heartbreaking change. Full-page illustrations enhance this bittersweet story of a princess who could never be queen.

The Lost Children

Paul Goble. Illustrated by the author. Bradbury. ISBN 0-02-736555-7. CC '94.

> This Blackfoot Indian legend tells of six mistreated brothers who finally escape their miserable life on earth and go to the Above World, where they become the Pleiades star group.

Macmillan Animal Encyclopedia for Children

Roger Few. Illustrated with full-color drawings and photographs. Macmillan. ISBN 0-02-762425-0. CC '92.

> "What I like about this book is that it shows all the animals that live in certain areas, like mountains, woods, deserts, and oceans," said one 5th grader. The book is arranged by natural habitat and explores the creatures that live in each and why.

The Magic School Bus on the Ocean Floor

Joanna Cole. Illustrated by Bruce Degen. Scholastic. ISBN 0-590-41430-5. CC '92.

> Another wonderful adventure with the ever-crazy teacher Ms. Frizzle. Readers will journey into the fascinating world of the ocean through cartoonlike illustrations loaded with facts and information.

Magnification

Beth B. Norden and Lynette Ruschak. Illustrated with photographs. Lodestar. ISBN 0-525-67417-9. CC '94.

> This lift-the-flap book is a winner. One student said "Wow, it shows everything up close, even a dust bunny!" Styrofoam, table salt, straight pins, an eyelash tip, and even a scab are magnified to get a real close look.

Make Four Million Dollar$ by Next Thur$day!

Stephen Manes. Illustrated by George Ulrich. Bantam. ISBN 0-533-07050-9. CC '92.

> When Jason finds the book *Make Four Million Dollar$ by Next Thur$day!* he is determined to follow the zany advice of the author, Dr. K. Pinkerton Silverfish. Will he become four million dollars richer? More importantly, can you?

Manatee: On Location

Kathy Darling. Photographs by Tara Darling. Lothrop, Lee & Shepard. ISBN 0-688-09030-3. CC '92.

> The large grass-eating mammal called the manatee is a slowly vanishing species. Photographs give the reader a bird's eye view of life under the sea with the manatee. The text is concise and easy to read.

Meet Addy

Connie Porter. Illustrated by Melodye Rosales. Pleasant Company. ISBN 1-56247-076-0. CC '94.

> "I would tell a friend this is a good book about a family escaping slavery. It is a sad and exciting book with a lot of history, and the best part is when the women give Addy and her mother shelter."

Meet Tricky Coyote!

Retold by Gretchen Will Mayo. Illustrated by Gretchen Will Mayo. Walker and Company. ISBN 0-8027-8198-5. CC '94.

> Mayo uses humor well in this collection of Native American folk tales in which the coyote tricks, or tries to trick, others.

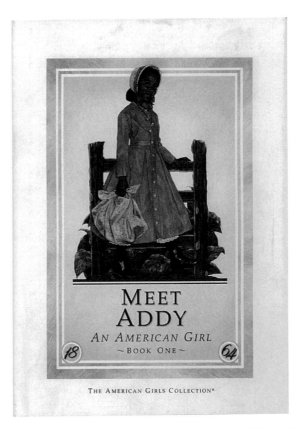

Cover illustration by Melodye Rosales from Connie Porter's Meet Addy.
©1993 by Pleasant Company Inc.

There are many lessons about human nature in these tales
from all sections of the United States.

Mind Twisters

Godfrey Hall. Illustrated by Peter Dennis, Linda Rodgers &
associates, and Oxford Illustrators. Random House. ISBN 0-
679-82038-8. CC '92.

> Puzzles and magic are apparent for almost all ages. All sub-
> jects are covered through tricks or other puzzles. If critical
> thinking is a priority, this book will entertain as well as stim-
> ulate the reader.

From The Moon Lady *by Amy Tan. Illustrations ©1992 by Gretchen Schields. Reprinted by permission of the Simon & Schuster Children's Publishing Division.*

The Moon of the Alligators

Jean Craighead George. Illustrated by Michael Rothman. HarperCollins. ISBN 0-06-022427-4. CC '92.

> An addition to the Thirteen Moons series, this book describes the ecosystem of the Florida Everglades by telling the story of one alligator and her search for food as the dry season begins. The lyrical prose incorporates superb wildlife illustrations.

The Moon of the Gray Wolves

Jean Craighead George. Illustrated by Sal Catalano. Harper-Collins. ISBN 0-06-022442-8. CC '92.

> This is one for the animal lover. Children will enjoy the author's story-like way of describing the life of the gray wolf in Alaska.

The Moon of the Mountain Lions

Jean Craighead George. Illustrated by Ron Parker. Harper-Collins. ISBN 0-06-022429-0. CC '92.

> Patterned after a Native American folk tale of night animals, this story shows us the mountain lion in the state of Washington but describes many animals of that region and their habits. An easy narrative style incorporates ecology and the balance of nature.

The Moon Lady

Amy Tan. Illustrated by Gretchen Schields. Macmillan. ISBN 0-02-78830-4. CC '92.

> An enthusiastic third grader commented, "I really loved this book because I learned about China and how people live there. Amy Tan's words really described how things looked, and the illustrations had such details. It made it all so real." You can really enjoy reading and learning from this story.

Mummies and Their Mysteries

Charlotte Wilcox. Illustrated with photographs. Carolrhoda Books. ISBN 0-87614-767-8. CC '94.

> An overview of mummies found all over the world. Clear, detailed text and striking photographs show how mummies provide information about the past. The section on the Americas, from Alaska to Peru, is very useful for units on these cultures. A good section on mummies buried in ice.

Nine O'Clock Lullaby

Marilyn Singer. Illustrated by Frané Lessac. HarperCollins. ISBN 0-06-025647-8. CC '92.

> Rich language and beautiful illustrations make this story about time zones and distant lands an excellent choice for language arts as well as content areas. It is a useful interdisciplinary addition to the classroom.

Of Swans, Sugarplums, and Satin Slippers: Ballet Stories for Children

Violette Verdy. Illustrated by Marcia Brown. Scholastic. ISBN 0-590-43484-5. CC '92.

> A short summary precedes each of six classical ballet stories containing magic and the themes of good and evil. Beautiful watercolors are included.

175 More Science Experiments to Amuse and Amaze Your Friends

Terry Cash, Steve Parker, and Barbara Taylor. Illustrated by Kuo Kang Chen and Peter Bull. Random House. ISBN 0-679-80390-4. CC '92.

> "You should get this book and try some of the tricks—I did!" one 5th grader commented. A sequel to *Experiments to Amuse and Amaze Your Friends*, this book contains a variety of illustrated, concise experiments on sound, electricity, simple chemistry, and weather.

One World

Michael Foreman. Illustrated by the author. Arcade. ISBN 1-55970-108-0. CC '92.

> Creating a microcosm from a tidal pool, children gradually see the delicate balance between humans and the environment. One 3rd grader commented, "It is a good book to remind people that we only have one world and we need to take care of it."

Our Solar System
Seymour Simon. Illustrated with photographs and diagrams. Morrow. ISBN 0-688-09992-0. CC '92.

> With an easy-to-read text, this award-winning author takes the reader on a fascinating tour of our solar system. Middle graders applaud its "great pictures and information." As an introduction to our amazing universe, it's a must!

Paper Magic: Creating Fantasies and Performing Tricks with Paper
Ormond McGill. Illustrated by Anne Canevari Green. Millbrook. ISBN 1-56294-136-4. CC '92.

> A guaranteed way to make an artist out of anyone. Easy-to-use directions create many beautiful, intricate designs, figures, and paper tricks. Excellent for rainy day activities or everyday art activities. Kids will love the magic tricks!

Pearl Harbor!
Wallace B. Black and Jean F. Blashfield. Crestwood House. ISBN 0-89686-555-X. CC '92.

> Actual photographs enhance a well written text about this major historical event and make it come alive.

The Random House Book of How Things Were Built
David J. Brown. Illustrated with full-color art and diagrams. Random House. ISBN 0-679-82044-2. CC '92.

> An X-ray look into 56 awesome and timeless structures like the Eiffel Tower, the Taj Mahal, the Great Pyramid, or the Great Wall of China makes structure design, engineering, and construction fascinating and very real. The colorful pictures are without equal.

The Rebellious Alphabet

Jorge Diaz. Illustrated by Oivind S. Jorfald. Holt. ISBN 0-8050-2765-3. CC '94.

> This far-fetched alphabet book, with detailed graphics and political ideas, has a definite message. An illiterate dictator bans all reading and writing, but an old man finds an ingenious way of bringing messages to the people.

The River

Gary Paulsen. Delacorte. ISBN 0-385-30388-2. CC '92.

> This is a "must read" for anyone who traveled with Brian Robeson on his terrifying adventures in the book *Hatchet*. Two years after Brian's first encounter with the wilderness, the government asks him to do it all again so others may learn from his survival techniques.

A River Ran Wild: An Environmental History

Lynne Cherry. Illustrated by the author. Gulliver/Harcourt Brace & Company. ISBN 0-15-200542-0. CC '92.

> The Hash-a-way River was a clean, sparkling river, an ideal home for Chief Weeawa's people. But "progress" changes all that. Then Oweana, a descendant of Weeawa, decides something must be done. A beautifully illustrated book to use for environmental units.

Shadow Theater: Games and Projects

Denny Robson and Vanessa Bailey. Illustrated with drawings and photographs. Franklin Watts. ISBN 0-531-17270-8. CC '92.

> A great book for students who want to use their imagination and creativity. Good collection of ways to make shadow characters come alive. Describes types of hand shadows and includes ways to make jointed puppets and a puppet theater.

Stephen Biesty's Cross-Sections: Man-of-War
Richard Platt. Illustrated by Stephen Biesty. Dorling Kindersley. ISBN 1-56458-321-X. CC '94.

> Artist Stephen Biesty has illustrated a section-by-section tour through a typical man-of-war of Great Britain's Royal Navy in about 1800. It contains intriguing drawings and details about the ship as well as the sailors.

Storm
Jenny Wood. Thomson Learning. ISBN 1-56847-002-9. CC '94.

> Part of the Violent Earth series, the book is divided into chapters explaining various kinds of storms. Illustrated with photos, charts, and graphs, it also discusses prediction and control. Included are a glossary and suggestions for further reading and projects.

Summer Wheels
Eve Bunting. Illustrated by Thomas B. Allen. Harcourt Brace & Company. ISBN 0-15-207000-1. CC '92.

> The bicycle man fixes up old bikes and lends them to neighborhood kids for free. "Anybody fool enough to give me something for nothing deserves to lose it," says the new kid who calls himself Abraham Lincoln. But he eventually does return the bike, using the only means he knows to get acceptance and friendship.

Vasilissa the Beautiful: A Russian Folktale
Adapted by Elizabeth Winthrop. Illustrated by Alexander Koshkin. HarperCollins. ISBN 0-06-021662-X. CC '92.

> A beautifully illustrated retelling of a Russian fairy tale about the beautiful Vasilissa and her struggles with her wicked stepmother and stepsisters. Vasilissa uses her magic doll to escape from the witch Baba Yaga. Children love this story reminiscent of "Cinderella" and "Hansel and Gretel."

Illustration by Thomas B. Allen from Eve Bunting's Summer Wheels. *Reprinted by permission of HBJ.*

Volcano

Christopher Lampton. Illustrated with color photographs. Millbrook. ISBN 1-56294-028-7. CC '92.

> "I really like disaster books," commented one 4th grader, "and the pictures in this one are great." Aberrations hold special interest for readers young and old, and this one has glossy photographs, color maps, charts, and a glossary to make it extra appealing.

Volcano!

Margaret Thomas. Crestwood House. ISBN 0-89686-595-9. CC '92.

> This well written nonfiction book describes some famous volcanic eruptions. Actual photographs and maps enhance the text.

Illustration from Vasilissa The Beautiful: A Russian Folktale *adapted by Elizabeth Winthrop. Illustration ©1991 by Alexander Koshkin. Reprinted by permission of HarperCollins Publishers.*

Walt Disney's Alice's Tea Party

Lyn Calder. Illustrated by Jesse Clay. Disney Press. ISBN 1-56282-145-8. CC '92.

> Middle readers find all that they need to know to throw their own Alice in Wonderland-style tea party. Activities, stories, recipes, and games are all based on the Disney version of this classic.

Water's Way

Lisa Westberg Peters. Illustrated by Ted Rand. Arcade. ISBN 1-55970-062-9. CC '92.

> Primary children enjoyed this easy-reading book about the different forms that water can have, from clouds to steam to fog. They loved the pictures.

Westward Ho Ho Ho! Jokes from the Wild West

Victoria Hartman. Illustrated by G. Brian Karas. Viking. ISBN 0-670-84040-8. CC '92.

> "What do you call a rush to the post office? A stamp-ede!" Vocabulary and humor are challenged as children read and interpret these jokes, puns, and plays on words. Funny illustrations provide clues for those who need a hand.

What's on the Menu? Food Poems

Selected by Bobbye Goldstein. Illustrated by Chris L. Demarest. Viking. ISBN 0-670-83031-3. CC '92.

> A delicious collection of poems that young readers will enjoy, from Jack Prelutsky's "Mother's Chocolate Valentine" to Rachel Field's "The Ice-Cream Man." Vivid and cartoonlike illustrations make this menu all the more inviting.

Where on Earth: A Geografunny Guide to the Globe

Paul Rosenthal. Illustrated by Marc Rosenthal. Knopf. ISBN 0-679-80833-7. CC '92.

> Children love the humorous presentation of this introduction to various aspects of geography. A lot of academic information is shared about each continent along with a running commentary offered in colored cartoons.

Wings

Jane Yolen. Illustrated by Dennis Nolan. HBJ. ISBN 0-15-297850-X. CC '92.

> Wings tells a Greek legend about Daedalus, a gifted craftsman, and his son Icarus. The story is filled with colorful details of the legend that revolves around pride. Beautiful, sensitive watercolors are featured.

Wonders of Science

Melvin Berger. Illustrated by G. Brian Karas. Scholastic. ISBN
0-590-43472-1. CC '92.

Fascinating facts about sound, light, water, heat, and air, cou-
pled with instructions for simple experiments that demon-
strate scientific principles, make this a gold mine of information. The hands-on approach and variety of projects invite
participation.

Worm's Eye View: Make Your Own Wildlife Refuge

Kipchak Johnson. Illustrated by Thompson Yardley. Millbrook. ISBN 1-878841-30-0. CC '92.

Tells how to make a wildlife refuge in your own backyard.
Colorful drawings "make the book look like it is a fiction
book, but the words are facts," analyzed one young reader.
"That's really why kids like it."

The Wretched Stone

Chris Van Allsburg. Illustrated by the author. Houghton
Mifflin. ISBN 0-395-53307-4. CC '92.

Vivid illustrations depict the events in this journal written by
the captain of the *Rita Ann*. An extraordinary glowing rock
that mysteriously turns sailors into monkeys makes this tale
mesmerizing.

Older Readers

All But Alice

Phyllis Reynolds Naylor. Atheneum. ISBN 0-689-31773-5. CC '92.

How do you become one of the "in" group in junior high? For Alice it's a full-time job, especially without a mom or sister to help her through the rough spots. Funny problems—realistic solutions.

Alone in the House

Edmund Plante. Avon. ISBN 0-380-76424-5. CC '92.

Sixteen-year-old Joanne is home alone when a mysterious stranger appears. Could he really be a vampire? One reader called it "a blood-curdling tale you can't put down." Another warns, "It's great, but don't read it before bed!"

Bully for You, Teddy Roosevelt!

Jean Fritz. Illustrated by Mike Wimmer. Putnam. ISBN 0-399-21769-X. CC '92.

The 26th U.S. president, Theodore Roosevelt, was a man of many causes and passions, not wanting to waste a minute. A well written biography about this colorful man who overcame illness to become everything from a politician to a conservationist.

Civil War! America Becomes One Nation

James I. Robertson, Jr. Illustrated with photos, prints, and maps. Knopf. ISBN 0-394-82996-4. CC '92.

> A captivating narrative enhanced by numerous maps and photographs takes young readers to the front line of the U.S. Civil War. "It makes the Civil War real. It's almost like being there," expressed a juvenile reader.

Coast to Coast

Betsy Byars. Bantam Doubleday Dell. ISBN 0-385-30787-X. CC '92.

> Readers experienced the thrills and relationship shared by two partners up in the air, facing the risks and the beauty of the cross-country flight that 13-year-old Birch and her grandfather take in his old Piper Cub.

The Courage of Magic Johnson

Peter Pascarelli. Bantam Doubleday Dell. ISBN 0-553-29915-8. CC '92.

> "It was amazing to see that Magic had problems on his basketball team even though he was the best player. He wasn't accepted until he learned to become a team player," wrote one seventh grader. The book reveals Magic's character and values, as well as his star qualities.

Crosstown

Kathryn Makris. Avon Flare. ISBN -0-380-76226-9. CC '94.

> Readers empathized with April, who was forced to move away from her comfortable home to a dingy apartment in another part of town. One girl added: "It tells about a teenager and what she thinks and goes through."

Did You Hear About Amber? Surviving 16 #1

Cherie Bennett. Puffin High Flyer. ISBN 0-14-036318-1. CC '94.

> Amber is from the wrong side of the tracks but still has everything going for her—a scholarship to a private school, the

richest, cutest boy, and her own dance trio. Why does her world seem to be falling apart?

Do Fishes Get Thirsty? Questions Answered by the New England Aquarium

Les Kaufman and the staff of the New England Aquarium. Illustrated with photographs. Franklin Watts. ISBN 0-531-15214-6. CC '92.

> Children loved the beautiful underwater photos in this book about the sea and its creatures. Here are the 26 questions that children most often ask. Some of the answers are very surprising.

Dogs Don't Tell Jokes

Louis Sachar. Knopf. ISBN 0-679-82017-5. CC '92.

> "Goon" longs to be accepted by his peers, but his continual joking alienates everyone. The school talent show is his last hope for fame and popularity. Or will he only make a fool of himself? Students commented, "It's hilarious," and "You can't put it down without a struggle."

Don't Blink Now! Capturing the Hidden World of Sea Creatures

Ann Downer. Illustrated with photographs. Franklin Watts. ISBN 0-531-15225-1. CC '92.

> Great underwater photographs of marine animals! Birth, growth, the hunt, and death are included. The reading complements the photographs with clear, precise information.

Exploring the Bismarck: The Real-Life Quest to Find Hitler's Greatest Battleship

Robert D. Ballard. Illustrated by Wesley Lowe, Ken Marshall, Jack McMaster, and Margo Stahl. Scholastic. ISBN 0-590-44268-6. CC '92.

> Oceanographers search the ocean floor for the battleship Bismarck, sunken 50 years ago. This story is told along with the

actual events that led to the disaster. "It gave me a feeling of what the war felt like."

Eyewitness Science: Light
David Burnie. Illustrated with photographs. Dorling Kindersley. ISBN 1-879431-79-3. CC '92.

> A creative layout, many color pictures, and easily understandable diagrams and text are used to explain the origins, principles, and historical study of light. The eye-appealing format encourages young and old to investigate the wonders of light.

Eyewitness Science: Matter
Christopher Cooper. Illustrated with photographs. Dorling Kindersley. ISBN 1-879431-88-2. CC '92.

> Quality photographs, drawings, and interesting tidbits of information about the whole spectrum of matter, including a historic perspective, caused even reluctant readers to pore over the text and long to own the book.

Finding Buck McHenry
Alfred Slote. HarperCollins. ISBN 0-06-021652-2. CC '92.

> Eleven-year-old Jason Ross suspects the school custodian Mack Henry might really be the great Buck McHenry, who pitched in the old Negro leagues back when black players were excluded from the majors. This story is a mystery tale, a sports novel, and a story of how one boy's life is touched by a legend.

Ghost Stories
Compiled by Robert Westall. Illustrated by Sean Eckett. Kingfisher Books. ISBN 1-85697-884-2. CC '94.

> Suspense and surprise are key ingredients in this collection of 21 stories from some of the world's best known writers. Witches, ghosts, and specters fill these tales of the supernatural. A sure hit for Halloween.

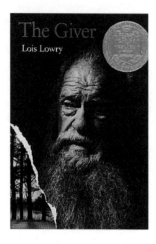

The Giver
Lois Lowry. Houghton Mifflin. ISBN 0-395-64566-2. CC '94.

> In this exciting science fiction novel, 12-year-old Jonas has received his lifetime assignment, an apprenticeship under his society's most important member, the Giver. Learning their shocking history forces Jonas to take extreme measures. An outstanding read-aloud and discussion generator.

Hakeem Olajuwon: Tower of Power
George R. Rekela. Illustrated with photographs. Lerner. ISBN 0-8225-0518-5. CC '94.

> This sports biography of the star center for the Houston Rockets is, as one youngster commented, "perfect if you're a basketball fanatic, like I am ."

Honey, I Blew Up the Kid
Adapted from the film by Todd Strasser. Illustrated with color stills from the film. Disney Press. ISBN 1-56282-204-7. CC '92.

> Just when you thought it was safe to leave Dad with the kids—Dad accidentally zaps his young son into a monster toddler. Las Vegas is terrorized before the process is reversed. Sequel to *Honey, I Shrunk the Kids*.

I Have a Dream: The Life and Words of Martin Luther King, Jr.

Jim Haskins. Illustrated with photographs. Millbrook. ISBN 1-56294-087-2. CC '92.

> This book on Martin Luther King, Jr., shares many pictures of the civil rights leader along with quotations from many speeches and writings. Also included are a list of sources, a chronology of his life, and the recollections of Rosa Parks in the introduction.

In-Line Skating: A Complete Guide for Beginners

George Sullivan. Illustrated with photographs. Cobblehill. ISBN 0-525-65124-1. CC '94.

> A colorful guide to one of the country's fastest growing sports, this introduction to in-line skating covers technique, safety, and care of equipment. A must for the novice in-line skater.

It Happened in America: True Stories from the Fifty States

Lila Perl. Illustrated by Ib Ohlsson. Holt. ISBN 0-8050-1719-4. CC '92.

> Not boring facts and statistics but a collection of fascinating tales from the 50 states. From the discovery of dinosaur bones to the construction of the first Ferris wheel, American legends and characters come to life in this gathering of stories

Illustration from In-Line Skating: A Complete Guide for Beginners *by George Sullivan. Copyright ©1993 Puffin Books.*

from U.S. history. To add to the enjoyment, each section is introduced with trivia questions sure to capture the imaginations of young readers.

The Jolly Christmas Postman
Janet and Allan Ahlberg. Illustrated by the authors. Little, Brown. ISBN 0-316-02033-8. CC '92.

> A jolly messenger, the Postman, makes his rounds at Christmas with a wonderful pouch overflowing with good cheer. Letters, puzzles, and even a book are tucked away into envelopes within this book.

The Jungle Book
Rudyard Kipling. Illustrated by Gregory Alexander. Arcade. ISBN 1-55970-127-7. CC '92.

> "Filled with wonderful adventure stories, and the paintings are exquisitely beautiful," wrote a young reader about this edition of a classic. Stories about Mowgli, the fearless man-cub, and Rikki-Tikki-Tavi, the cobra-battling mongoose, still enthrall children today.

The Kingfisher Illustrated Encyclopedia of Animals
Edited by Michael Chinery. Illustrated with over 100 color photographs, illustrations, and diagrams. Kingfisher Books. ISBN 1-85697-801-X. CC '92.

> Older readers delight in this introduction to more than 2,000 animals. With vivid color photographs and drawings, it provides a quick introduction to species size, habitat, and behavior.

Kirby Puckett: Fan Favorite
Ann Bauleke. Illustrated with photographs. Lerner. ISBN 0-8225-0490-1. CC '94.

> Kirby Puckett's biography turned readers' thoughts to baseball. "This was a story about a man who was more than I thought he was," wrote one enthusiastic student.

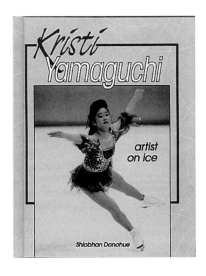

Cover illustration from Shiobhan Donohue's Kristi Yamaguchi: Artist on Ice. *©1994 by Lerner Publications Company.*

Kriss Kross Krazy!

Anne Raso. Bantam Doubleday Dell. ISBN 0-553-56179-0. CC '92.

> The story of teenage rappers Chris Kelly and Chris Smith, who were discovered while shopping at a mall. Despite their success, they still try to live average lives and excel in school. As Chris Smith's dad said, "The pen is lighter than the shovel."

Kristi Yamaguchi: Artist on Ice

Shiobhan Donohue. Illustrated with photographs. Lerner. ISBN 0-8225-0522-3. CC '94.

> Dreams come true in this well organized biography of champion figure skater Kristi Yamaguchi. An index of figure skating terms and moves clarifies the language of ice-skating. An entertaining and informative book for sports enthusiasts and future Olympic hopefuls.

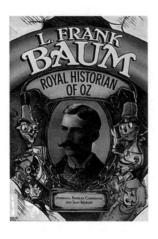

Cover illustration from L. Frank Baum: Royal Historian of Oz *by Angelica Shirley Carpenter and Jean Shirley. Text ©1992 by Angelica Shirley Carpenter and Jean Shirley; photographs and illustrations ©1992 by Lerner Publications Company. Reprinted by permission of Lerner Publications Company.*

Letting Swift River Go
Jane Yolen. Illustrated by Barbara Cooney. Little, Brown. ISBN 0-316-96899-4. CC '92.

> A nostalgic, picturesque tale of changing times in parts of the rural northeastern United States. A personal view of the way things were before the flooding of Swift River towns to create the freshwater Quabbin Reservoir. Delightful full-page illustrations highlight the story.

L. Frank Baum: Royal Historian of Oz
Angelica Shirley Carpenter and Jean Shirley. Illustrated with photographs. Lerner. ISBN 0-8225-4910-7. CC '92.

> The yellow brick road was not always easy for L. Frank Baum, author of *The Wizard of Oz*. Older students appreciate this realistic glimpse into the life of the Oz creator.

The Los Angeles Riots: America's Cities in Crisis
John Salak. Illustrated with photographs. Millbrook. ISBN 1-56294-373-1. CC '94.

> On April 29, 1992, an urban riot, ignited by a not-guilty verdict in the Rodney King trial, exploded in Los Angeles, California. This well organized view of urban unrest details the King incident, its aftermath, and the many social crises that

can provoke urban violence. An excellent source for reports on urban issues.

The Magic: Earvin Johnson
Bill Morgan. Scholastic. ISBN 0-590-46050-1. CC '92.

Most people have heard of Magic Johnson's remarkable abilities on the basketball court. Now you can read about his incredible life and the qualities that have made him a legend off the court.

Malcolm X: Black Rage
David Collins. Illustrated with photographs. Dillon Press. ISBN 0-87518-498-7. CC '92.

This biography reads like a feature on the evening news. A character study, the book chronicles Malcolm Little's life, from a broken home to his involvement with drugs, his prison term where he became a voracious reader, and finally to Malcolm X, one of the most controversial civil rights leaders of our time.

Cover illustration from David R. Collins's Malcolm X: Black Rage. *©1992 by David R. Collins. Reprinted by permission of Dillon Press.*

Mama, Let's Dance

Patricia Hermes. Little, Brown. ISBN 0-316-35861-4. CC '92.

> Mary Belle tells the story of abandoned children who survive on their own. Middle-school students were affected by this book and asked, "How could a mother do this to her children? How could they be so self-sufficient?"

Mission from Mount Yoda. Star Wars #4

Paul Davids and Hollace Davids. Illustrated by June Brigman and Karl Kesel. Skylark/Bantam Doubleday Dell. ISBN 0-553-15890-2. CC '94.

> The adventure continues as Ken gets trapped in the cargo hold of the spaceship. Will they get past the giant Fefze beetles to the Valley of Royalty in time to save the treasure from being stolen by Kadann?

Moonshiner's Son

Carolyn Reeder. Macmillan. ISBN 0-02-775805-2. CC '94.

> Tom Higgins, a 12-year-old in Virginia's Blue Ridge Mountains, is learning the art of making whiskey. Readers anxiously anticipate how Tom and his father escape law officers sent by the new preacher. All goes well until tragedy strikes.

My Co-Star, My Enemy. Hollywood Wars #1

Ilene Cooper. Puffin High Flyer. ISBN 0-14-036156-1. CC '94.

> "It was about the Hollywood wars between two girls who are always fighting about something, like how they are supposed to act and dress, and about their boyfriends. It was really great!"

Nightjohn

Gary Paulsen. Illustrated by Jerry Pinkney. Delacorte/Bantam
Doubleday Dell. ISBN 0-385-30838-8. CC '94.

> Not for the faint hearted, this historically accurate account of
> the U.S. South in 1850 reveals the brutal treatment of slaves,
> especially when they attempt escape and are caught teaching
> other slaves to read. One seventh grader commented that
> "Gary Paulsen makes things seem so real."

Cover illustration from
Nightjohn. *Copyright ©1993
by Gary Paulsen. Jacket
illustration ©1993 by Jerry
Pinkney. Reprinted by
permission of Bantam
Doubleday Dell.*

On the Tracks of Dinosaurs: A Study of Dinosaur Footprints
James O. Farlow. Illustrated by Doris Tischler. Franklin Watts. ISBN 0-531-15220-0. CC '92.

>Even students who think they know about dinosaurs are fascinated as Farlow's photographs, diagrams, and descriptions reveal how the reptiles' footprints were fossilized, how scientists study them, and what new ideas they suggest about dinosaur behavior.

People in Art
Anthea Peppin. Illustrated with photographs and reproductions. Millbrook. ISBN 1-56294-171-2. CC '92.

>This book focuses on people in art and uses examples of famous works of art for activities and projects for the young artist. "I loved the idea of making a life-sized figure," a younger reader commented. Profusely illustrated.

Rising Voices: Writings of Young Native Americans
Selected by Arlene B. Hirshfelder and Beverly R. Singer. Scribner's. ISBN 0-684-19207-1. CC '92.

>This collection of essays and poems discloses the thoughts of young Native Americans trying to balance between the traditional and modern worlds. The selections are thoughtful and often moving.

Rosa Parks: My Story
Rosa Parks with Jim Haskins. Illustrated with photographs. Dial. ISBN 0-8037-0673-1. CC '92.

>Rosa Parks gives us a new look at the events that shaped her character, causing her to serve a pivotal role in the 1955 bus boycott in Montgomery, Alabama. Rosa's dignity and candor shine throughout her story, making her a fine role model for young people.

Roseanne Arnold: Comedy's Queen Bee
Katherine E. Krohn. Illustrated with photographs. Lerner.
ISBN 0-8225-0520-7. CC '94.

> Roseanne's biography appealed to her many fans who wanted
> to know more about their favorite star. One found it "funny—
> just like a comedy show."

Saving Endangered Mammals: A Field Guide to Some of the Earth's Rarest Animals
Thane Maynard. Illustrated with photographs. Franklin
Watts. ISBN 0-531-15253-7. CC '92.

> Did you know that the Philippine tarsier's existence is threat-
> ened by logging? The okapi, the only living relative of the
> giraffe, is in danger of extinction from poaching. Beautiful
> photographs accompany facts about 30 endangered animals.

Scary Stories 3: More Tales to Chill Your Bones
Collected and retold by Alvin Schwartz. Illustrated by
Stephen Gammell. HarperCollins. ISBN 0-06-021794-4. CC
'92.

> By popular request, here is another collection of terrifying
> tales, including at least one true story, to thrill youngsters.
> The notes and sources give interesting background, and
> Stephen Gammell's drawings set the scene perfectly. "It
> might scare you," a reader warns.

The Secrets of Vesuvius: Exploring the Mysteries of an Ancient Buried City
Sara C. Bisel. Illustrated with photographs. Scholastic. ISBN 0-
590-43850-6. CC '92.

> Part fact, part historical fiction, an archaeologist and anthro-
> pologist reconstructs the events of a small beachfront com-
> munity the day before Mount Vesuvius erupted. Her story is
> based on excavations of bones and artifacts of the Roman
> town.

Ships: Sailors and the Sea
Richard Humble. Illustrated by Mark Bergin, Bill Donohoe, Nick Hewetson, Tony Townsend, Hans Wilborg-Jenssen, and Gerald Wood. Franklin Watts. ISBN 0-531-15234-0. CC '92.

> The surgeon's chest "had a mallet for knocking out the patient before operating on him." Other tidbits intrigue readers on a voyage through the history of ships. Every page has illustrations, and children like it "because it has good pictures."

The Sierra Club Book of Great Mammals
Linsay Knight. Illustrated with full-color photographs and art. Sierra Club. ISBN 0-87156-507-2. CC '92.

> A brief overview of mammals, their origins, and characteristics, followed by informative text and colorful, detailed photographs of 19 groups of great mammals. Valuable as a resource, this book also appeals to readers who simply want to find out more about the larger mammal species.

The Sierra Club Book of Weatherwisdom
Vicki McVey. Illustrated by Martha Weston. Sierra Club/ Little, Brown. ISBN 0-316-56341-2. CC '92.

> Climates and seasons, wind and rain, warm and cold fronts, atmospheric pressure, and weather predictions are discussed in this interesting book of weather. There are hands-on activities, games, and experiments. This book makes weather fun to learn.

Sluggers! Twenty-Seven of Baseball's Greatest
George Sullivan. Illustrated with photographs. Atheneum. ISBN 0-689-31566-X. CC '92.

> Here are 27 of the greatest sluggers of all time. Starting today with the likes of Jose Canseco and stretching back to players like Roger Connor, Sullivan brings each player to life and describes his amazing achievements.

Somewhere Between Life and Death

Lurlene McDaniel. Bantam. ISBN 0-553-28349-9. CC '92.

> The drama group's cast party wasn't supposed to end in tragedy. However, Amy has a horrible car accident and lies in a coma. Her parents and her sister Erin must find the courage to accept that Amy's life-support systems will never bring her back.

Spill! The Story of the Exxon Valdez

Terry Carr. Illustrated with photographs. Franklin Watts. ISBN 0-531-15217-0. CC '92.

> Color photographs enhance this account of the worst oil spill in American history. As a reader noted, "It has pictures of everything it talked about." Chapters titled "Collision," and "Harvest of Death" make it a page turner.

Sports Cards

Robert Young. Dillon Press. ISBN 0-87518-519-3. CC '94.

> An excellent introduction into the hobby of sports card collecting, including the history, production, and collecting of sports-related trading cards. A fascinating way to gain knowledge of a particular area.

The Super Book of Baseball

Ron Berler. Illustrated with photographs. Sports Illustrated for Kids. ISBN 0-316-09240-1. CC '92.

> Berler goes beyond the typical endless lists of statistics and encapsulates a broad range of baseball's memorable events, teams, and individual players' stories. Hundreds of old and modern photographs bring to life the history of "America's favorite pastime" for young readers.

Thirteen: 13 Tales of Horror by 13 Masters of Horror

Edited by Tonya Pines. Scholastic. ISBN 0-590-45256-8. CC '92.

> Here are 13 horror stories from favorite authors such as Christopher Pike and R.L. Stine. Eighth graders thought it was "chilling and suspenseful. It is a very scary book to read at night."

Unsolved! Famous Real-Life Mysteries

George Sullivan. Scholastic. ISBN 0-590-42990-6. CC '92.

> "It's really gory" is the comment made by a 7th grade girl as she finished this book of real-life stories of disappearing children, unsolved murders, and airplane crashes in midair. The perfect book for real mystery lovers.

What Daddy Did

Neal Shusterman. Little, Brown. ISBN 0-316-78906-2. CC '92.

> A moving and emotional novel "about love even through bad times," wrote one student. No matter what Preston does, he always come back to the same question—"Is it all right to kill?"

The Worst Day I Ever Had

Fred McMane and Cathrine Wolf. Photographs by Brad Hamann. Sports Illustrated for Kids. ISBN 0-316-55354-9. CC '92.

> Everyone has bad days, even heroes. This book highlights 13 sports figures and one of the adversities each had to face in his or her career. This book helps to satisfy children's desire for more information about favorite athletes.

Author and Illustrator Index

Bang, Molly, Marcia Brown, Barbara Cooney, Donald Crews, Leo
 Dillon, Diane Dillon, Richard Egielski, Trina Schart Hyman, Anita
 Lobel, Jerry Pinkney, John Schoenherr, Marc Simont, Chris Van
 Allsburg, David Wiesner, and Ed Young (Illustrators). *From Sea to
 Shining Sea: A Treasury of American Folklore and Folk Songs.* (1994). 7
Barasch, Marc Ian. *No Plain Pets!* (1992). 45
Barnidge, Tom (Editor). *Good Days, Bad Days: An Official NFL Book.*
 (1993). 7
Bauer, Nancy (Illustrator). *Belly's Deli.* (1994). 4
—— (Illustrator). *Mrs. Bretsky's Bakery.* (1994). 12
Bauleke, Ann. *Kirby Puckett: Fan Favorite.* (1994). 88
Becker, Antoinette (Illustrator). *Best Friends.* (1994). 62
Bennett, Cherie. *Did You Hear About Amber? Surviving 16 #1.* (1994). 83
Berger, Melvin. *Wonders of Science.* (1992). 81
Bergin, Mark, Bill Donohoe, Nick Hewetson, John James, Tony
 Townsend, Hans Wilborg-Jenssen, and Gerald Wood (Illustrators).
 Inventions: Inventors & Ingenious Ideas. (1993). 68
Bergin, Mark, Bill Donohoe, Nick Hewetson, Tony Townsend, Hans
 Wilborg-Jenssen, and Gerald Wood. (Illustrators). *Ships: Sailors and
 the Sea.* (1992). 96
Berlan, Kathryn Hook. *Andrew's Amazing Monsters.* (1994). 27
Berler, Ron. *The Super Book of Baseball.* (1992). 97
Bernardini, Robert. *A Southern Time Christmas.* (1992). 14
Biegel, Michael David (Illustrator). *Jesse Owens: Olympic Star.* (1993).
 68
Biesty, Stephen (Illustrator). *Incredible Cross-Sections.* (1993). 8–9
—— (Illustrator). *Stephen Biesty's Cross-Sections: Man-of-War.* (1994). 77
Birkinshaw, Linda (Illustrator). *It Was a Dark and Stormy Night.* (1992).
 9
Biro, Val (Illustrator). *When I Was Your Age.* (1992). 16
Bisel, Sara C. *The Secrets of Vesuvius: Exploring the Mysteries of an Ancient
 Buried City.* (1992). 95
Black, Wallace B., and Jean F. Blashfield. *Pearl Harbor!* (1992). 75
Blashfield, Jean F. (*see* Black, Wallace B.)
Blishen, Edward (Selector). *Children's Classics to Read Aloud.* (1993). 6
Bolton, Linda. *Hidden Pictures.* (1994). 8
Bond, Felicia (Illustrator). *If You Give a Moose a Muffin.* (1992). 40
Bowden, Joan. *Planes of the Aces: A Three-Dimensional Collection of the
 Most Famous Aircraft in the World.* (1994). 13
Braybrooks, Ann (Film writer). *Walt Disney's 101 Dalmatians: Illustrated
 Classic.* (1992). 16
Brett, Jan. *Trouble with Trolls.* (1993). 55
Bridwell, Norman. *Clifford, We Love You.* (1992). 32

ments to Amuse and Amaze Your Friends. (1992). 74

Chen, Kuo Kang, and others (Illustrators). *175 Amazing Nature Experiments*. (1993). 13

Cherry, Lynne. *A River Ran Wild: An Environmental History*. (1993). 76

Chinery, Michael (Editor). *The Kingfisher Illustrated Encyclopedia of Animals*. (1993). 88

Christelow, Eileen. *Don't Wake Up Mama! Another Five Little Monkeys Story*. (1993). 35

———. *Five Little Monkeys Sitting in a Tree*. (1992). 19

Clay, Wil (Illustrator). *Tailypo!* (1992). 15

Clay, Jesse. *Walt Disney's Alice's Tea Party*. (1993). 79

Clementson, John (Illustrator). *How Giraffe Got Such a Long Neck... And Why Rhino Is So Grumpy*. (1994). 40

Cohn, Amy L. (Compiler). *From Sea to Shining Sea: A Treasury of American Folklore and Folk Songs*. (1994). 7

Cole, Joanna. *The Magic School Bus on the Ocean Floor*. (1993). 69

Collins, David. *Malcolm X: Black Rage*. (1993). 91

Compton, Kenn, and Joanne Compton. *Granny Greenteeth and the Noise in the Night*. (1994). 39

Compton, Kenn (Illustrator). *Granny Greenteeth and the Noise in the Night*. (1994). 39

Compton, Joanne (*see* Compton, Kenn)

Conley, Andrea. *Window on the Deep: The Adventures of Underwater Explorer Sylvia Earle*. (1992). 17

Cooney, Barbara (*see* Bang, Molly)

——— (Illustrator). *Letting Swift River Go*. (1993). 90

Cooper, Christopher. *Eyewitness Science: Matter*. (1993). 85

Cooper, Ilene. *My Co-Star, My Enemy. Hollywood Wars #1*. (1994). 92

Cornell, Laura (Illustrator). *When I Was Little: A Four-Year-Old's Memoir of Her Youth*. (1994). 25

Crews, Donald (*see* Bang, Molly)

Cummings, Pat (Compiler and editor). *Talking with Artists*. (1993). 15

Curtis, Jamie Lee. *When I Was Little: A Four-Year-Old's Memoir of Her Youth*. (1994). 25

Cushman, Doug (Illustrator). *An Alligator Named...Alligator*. (1992). 26

Cuyler, Margery. *That's Good! That's Bad!* (1992). 53

Dakos, Kalli. *Don't Read This Book, Whatever You Do! More Poems About School*. (1994). 65

Darling, Kathy. *Manatee: On Location*. (1992). 70

Darling, Tara (Photographer). *Manatee: On Location*. (1992). 70

David, Rosalie. *The Giant Book of the Mummy*. (1994). 66

Davids, Paul, and Hollace Davids. *Mission from Mount Yoda. Star Wars*

Footprints. (1992). 94

Faulkner, Matt. *The Moon Clock*. (1992). 43

Few, Roger. *Macmillan Animal Encyclopedia for Children*. (1992). 69

Firth, Barbara (Illustrator). *The Grumpalump*. (1992). 39

Fleming, Denise. *In the Tall, Tall Grass*. (1992). 22

Fletcher, Helen Jill (crafts). *How on Earth Do We Recycle Paper?* (1993). 67

Foreman, Michael. *The Boy Who Sailed with Columbus*. (1993). 63

——. *One World*. (1992). 74

Fritz, Jean. *Bully for You, Teddy Roosevelt!* (1992). 82

——. *George Washington's Mother*. (1993). 38

Fuhr, Ute, and Raoul Sautai (Illustrators). *Whales: A First Discovery Book*. (1994). 57

Fuhr, Ute (*see* Jeunesse, Gallimard)

Gammell, Stephen (Illustrator). *Monster Mama*. (1994). 12

—— (Illustrator). *Old Black Fly*. (1993). 12–13

—— (Illustrator). *Scary Stories 3: More Tales to Chill Your Bones*. (1992). 95

Garns, Allen (Illustrator). *Gonna Sing My Head Off!* (1993). 7

George, Jean Craighead. *The Moon of the Alligators*. (1992). 72

——. *The Moon of the Gray Wolves*. (1992). 73

——. *The Moon of the Mountain Lions*. (1992). 73

Gibbons, Gail. *Whales*. (1992). 16

Goble, Paul. *The Lost Children*. (1994). 69

Goldstein, Bobbye (Selector). *What's on the Menu? Food Poems*. (1993). 80

Goode, Diane. *Diane Goode's Book of Silly Stories & Songs*. (1993). 33

Goodman, Beth (Adaptor). *Bingo*. (1992). 62

Gordon, Jeffie Ross. *Two Badd Babies*. (1993). 55

Gorman, Carol. *Die For Me*. (1993). 64

Graham-Barber, Lynda. *Gobble! The Complete Book of Thanksgiving Words*. (1992). 7

Grambling, Lois G. *An Alligator Named...Alligator*. (1992). 26

Greaves, Margaret. *Henry's Wild Morning*. (1992). 40

Green, Anne Canevari (Illustrator). *Paper Magic: Creating Fantasies and Performing Tricks with Paper*. (1993). 75

Greenblat, Rodney A. *Slombo the Gross*. (1994). 52

Greene, Katherine, and Richard Greene. *The Man Behind the Magic: The Story of Walt Disney*. (1992). 10

Greene, Richard (*see* Greene, Katherine)

Greene, Carol. *The Old Ladies Who Liked Cats*. (1992). 13

Groves, Seli (text). *How on Earth Do We Recycle Paper?* (1993). 67

Gutman, Bill. *David Robinson: NBA Super Center*. (1994). 64

Gwynne, Fred. *Easy to See Why*. (1994). 19

Hall, Godfrey. *Mind Twisters*. (1993). 71
Hamann, Brad (Photographer). *The Worst Day I Ever Had*. (1992). 98
Harlow, Rosie, and Gareth Morgan. *175 Amazing Nature Experiments*. (1993). 13
Harris, Nick, and Roger Stewart. (Illustrators). *The Giant Book of the Mummy*. (1994). 66
Harrison, David L. *Somebody Catch My Homework*. (1994). 14
Hartman, Victoria. *Westward Ho Ho Ho! Jokes from the Wild West*. (1993). 80
Haskins, Jim (*see* Parks, Rosa)
——. *I Have a Dream: The Life and Words of Martin Luther King, Jr*. (1993). 87
Hawkes, Kevin (Illustrator). *Hey, Hay! A Wagonful of Funny Homonym Riddles*. (1992). 8
Hawkins, Colin, and Jacqui Hawkins. *Knock! Knock!* (1992). 10
Hawkins, Jacqui (*see* Hawkins, Colin)
Hawkins, Colin (Illustrator). *Knock! Knock!* (1992). 10
Hayes, Sarah. *The Grumpalump*. (1992). 39
Hearn, Diane Dawson. *Dad's Dinosaur Day*. (1994). 33
Heiferman, Marvin (*see* Wegman, William)
Hermes, Patricia. *Mama, Let's Dance*. (1992). 92
Hewetson, Nick (*see* Bergin, Mark)
Hewett, Joan. *Tiger, Tiger, Growing Up*. (1994). 54
Hewett, Richard (Photographer). *Tiger, Tiger, Growing Up*. (1994). 54
Hicks, Russell (Illustrator). *Walt Disney's 101 Dalmatians: A Counting Book*. (1992). 25
Higginson, William J. (Editor). *Wind in the Long Grass: A Collection of Haiku*. (1992). 17
Hirshfelder, Arlene B., and Beverly R. Singer (Selectors). *Rising Voices: Writings of Young Native Americans*. (1993). 94
Hoffman, Rosekrans (Illustrator). *Jane Yolen's Mother Goose Songbook*. (1993). 9
Holleyman, Sonia. *Mona the Brilliant*. (1994). 43
——. *Mona the Vampire*. (1992). 43
Houston, Gloria. *My Great-Aunt Arizona*. (1993). 44
Hulme, Joy N. *Sea Squares*. (1992). 50
Humble, Richard. *Ships: Sailors and the Sea*. (1992). 96
Hyman, Trina Schart (*see* Bang, Molly)

James, J. Alison (Translator). *The Rainbow Fish*. (1993). 48
James, John (*see* Bergin, Mark)

James, Simon. *Dear Mr. Blueberry.* (1992). 33
——. *My Friend Whale.* (1992). 23
Jaspersohn, William. *Cranberries.* (1992). 32
Jennings, Linda. *The Dog Who Found Christmas.* (1994). 35
Jeunesse, Gallimard, Claude Delafosse, and René Mettler (Creators). *Birds: A First Discovery Book.* (1994). 4
Jeunesse, Gallimard, Claude Delafosse, C. Millet, and D. Millet (Creators). *Castles: A First Discovery Book.* (1994). 31
Jeunesse, Gallimard, Claude Delafosse, Ute Fuhr, and Raoul Sautai (Creators). *Whales: A First Discovery Book.* (1994). 57
Johnson, Kipchak. *Worm's Eye View: Make Your Own Wildlife Refuge.* (1992). 81
Johnson, Steve (Illustrator). *The Frog Prince Continued.* (1992). 6
Johnson, Neil. *The Battle of Lexington and Concord.* (1993). 62
Johnson, Meredith (Illustrator). *The Bathwater Gang Gets Down to Business: A Springboard Book.* (1993). 29
—— (Illustrator). *The Sub.* (1994). 52
Jones, Charlotte Foltz. *Mistakes That Worked.* (1992). 11
Jones, Frances. *Nature's Deadly Creatures: A Pop-Up Exploration.* (1993). 12
Jorfald, Oivind S. (Illustrator). *The Rebellious Alphabet.* (1994). 76

Karas, G. Brian (Illustrator). *Don't Read This Book, Whatever You Do! More Poems About School.* (1994). 65
—— (Illustrator). *The Holiday Handwriting School.* (1992). 40
—— (Illustrator). *Westward Ho Ho Ho! Jokes from the Wild West.* (1993). 80
—— (Illustrator). *Wonders of Science.* (1992). 81
Kaufman, Les, and the staff of the New England Aquarium. *Alligators to Zooplankton: A Dictionary of Water Babies.* (1992). 60
——. *Do Fishes Get Thirsty? Questions Answered by the New England Aquarium.* (1992). 84
Kelley, True (Illustrator). *Dinostory.* (1992). 34
Kellogg, Steven. *The Christmas Witch.* (1993). 31
—— (Reteller). *Jack and the Beanstalk.* (1992). 9
—— (Illustrator). *Parents in the Pigpen, Pigs in the Tub.* (1994). 13
Kennedy, X.J. *The Kite That Braved Old Orchard Beach.* (1992). 68
Kerrod, Robin. *The Children's Space Atlas.* (1993). 63
Kesel, Karl (*see* Brigman, June)
Kimmel, Eric A. (Reteller). *Anansi Goes Fishing.* (1993). 26
King, Deborah. *Custer.* (1993). 63
Kinsey, Helen (*see* Kinsey-Warnock, Natalie)
Kinsey-Warnock, Natalie, and Helen Kinsey. *The Bear That Heard*

Pig. (1994). 54

Oxford Illustrators (*see* Dennis, Peter)

Palmer, Jan (Illustrator). *Happy Thanksgiving Rebus.* (1992). 21

Parker, Ron (Illustrator). *The Moon of the Mountain Lions.* (1992). 73

Parker, Steve. *Inside the Whale and Other Animals.* (1993). 41

—— (*see* Cash, Terry)

Parks, Rosa, with Jim Haskins. *Rosa Parks: My Story.* (1993). 94

Pascarelli, Peter. *The Courage of Magic Johnson.* (1993). 83

Pastor, Terry (Illustrator). *The A-to-Z Book of Cars.* (1992). 60

Paton, John (Editor). *The Kingfisher Children's Encyclopedia.* (1993). 9

Paul, Korky (Illustrator). *Mrs. Wolf.* (1994). 43

Paulsen, Gary. *Dogteam.* (1994). 64

——. *Nightjohn.* (1994). 93

——. *The River.* (1992). 76

Paulsen, Ruth Wright (Illustrator). *Dogteam.* (1994). 64

Pearce, Fred. *The Big Green Book.* (1992). 4

Pelta, Kathy. *Discovering Christopher Columbus: How History Is Invented.* (1992). 64

Peppin, Anthea. *People in Art.* (1993). 94

Perl, Lila. *It Happened in America: True Stories from the Fifty States.* (1993). 87–88

Perlman, Janet (Reteller and Illustrator). *Cinderella Penguin.* (1994). 32

Perols, Sylvaine (Illustrator). *The Earth and Sky.* (1993). 65

Peters, Lisa Westberg. *Water's Way.* (1992). 79

Petersen, P.J. *The Sub.* (1994). 52

Pfister, Marcus. *The Rainbow Fish.* (1993). 48

Pilham, David. *Sam's Surprise.* (1993). 49

Pilkey, Dav. *Dragon's Fat Cat.* (1993). 36

Pinczes, Elinor J. *One Hundred Hungry Ants.* (1994). 46

Pines, Tonya (Editor). *Thirteen: 13 Tales of Horror by 13 Masters of Horror.* (1992). 98

Pinkney, Jerry (Illustrator). *Nightjohn.* (1994). 93

—— (*see* Bang, Molly)

Plante, Edmund. *Alone in the House.* (1992). 82

Platt, Richard. *Incredible Cross-Sections.* (1993). 8–9

——. *Stephen Biesty's Cross-Sections: Man-of-War.* (1994). 77

Polacco, Patricia. *Chicken Sunday.* (1993). 5

——. *Mrs. Katz and Tush.* (1993). 43

——. *Some Birthday!* (1992). 52

Porter, Connie. *Meet Addy.* (1994). 70

Potter, Katherine. *My Mother the Cat.* (1994). 45

Prelutsky, Jack (Selector). *For Laughing Out Loud: Poems to Tickle Your*

Sachar, Louis. *Dogs Don't Tell Jokes.* (1992). 84
——. *Monkey Soup.* (1993). 22
Salak, John. *The Los Angeles Riots: America's Cities in Crisis.* (1994). 90–91
Sandford, John (Illustrator). *Siegfried.* (1992). 51
Sautai, Raoul (*see* Jeunesse, Gallimard)
—— (*see* Fuhr, Ute)
Savage, Stephen. *Making Tracks: A Slide-and-See Book.* (1993). 10
Schanzer, Rosalyn. *Ezra in Pursuit: The Great Maze Chase.* (1994). 37
Schields, Gretchen (Illustrator). *The Moon Lady.* (1993). 73
Schindel, John. *Who Are You?* (1992). 58
Schindler, S.D. (Illustrator). *Big Pumpkin.* (1993). 18
—— (Illustrator). *Not the Piano, Mrs. Medley!* (1992). 12
Schoenherr, John (*see* Bang, Molly)
Schwartz, Alvin (Collector). *And the Green Grass Grew All Around: Folk Poetry from Everyone.* (1993). 3
—— (Collector and reteller). *Scary Stories 3: More Tales to Chill Your Bones.* (1992). 95
Schwartz, Carol (Illustrator). *Sea Squares.* (1992). 50
Scieszka, Jon. *The Frog Prince Continued.* (1992). 6
——. *The Stinky Cheese Man and Other Fairly Stupid Tales.* (1993). 14
Seiden, Art (Illustrator). *How on Earth Do We Recycle Paper?* (1993). 67
Serfozo, Mary. *Benjamin Bigfoot.* (1994). 29
Shafner, R.L., and Eric Jon Weisberg. *Belly's Deli.* (1994). 4
——. *Mrs. Bretsky's Bakery.* (1994). 12
Shannon, Margaret. *Elvira.* (1994). 36–37
Shaw, Nancy. *Sheep in a Shop.* (1992). 23–24
——. *Sheep Out To Eat.* (1993). 24
Shields, Carol Diggory. *I Am Really a Princess.* (1994). 8
Shirley, Jean (*see* Carpenter, Angelica Shirley)
Shusterman, Neal. *What Daddy Did.* (1992). 98
Silverman, Erica. *Big Pumpkin.* (1993). 18
Simon, Seymour. *Our Solar System.* (1993). 75
Simont, Marc (*see* Bang, Molly)
Singer, Marilyn. *Nine O'Clock Lullaby.* (1992). 74
Singer, Beverly R. (*see* Hirshfelder, Arlene B.)
Siracusa, Catherine. *The Giant Zucchini.* (1994). 20
Skilbeck, Clare (Illustrator). *Dinosaurs at the Supermarket.* (1994). 33
Slater, Teddy (Reteller). *Walt Disney's Mickey and the Beanstalk.* (1994). 55
Slote, Alfred. *Finding Buck McHenry.* (1992). 85
Smath, Jerry (Illustrator). *Seven Little Hippos.* (1992). 50–51

Smith, Tony, and Andrew Robinson (Illustrators). *Nature's Deadly Creatures: A Pop-Up Exploration*. (1993). 12

Smith, Lane (Illustrator). *The Stinky Cheese Man and Other Fairly Stupid Tales*. (1993). 14

Smith, Cat Bowman (Illustrator). *Monkey Soup*. (1993). 22

Smith, Jos. A. (Illustrator). *Benjamin Bigfoot*. (1994). 29

Speidel, Sandra (Illustrator). *Wind in the Long Grass: A Collection of Haiku*. (1992). 17

Spineli, Jerry. *Fourth Grade Rats*. (1992). 65

Spinelli, Eileen. *Somebody Loves You, Mr. Hatch*. (1992). 14

Spinelli, Jerry. *The Bathwater Gang Gets Down to Business: A Springboard Book*. (1993). 29

Stahl, Margo (*see* Lowe, Wesley)

Stanley, Diane. *Siegfried*. (1992). 51

—— (Illustrator). *The Last Princess: The Story of Princess Ka'iulani of Hawai'i*. (1992). 69

Stanley, Fay. *The Last Princess: The Story of Princess Ka'iulani of Hawai'i*. (1992). 69

Steig, William. *Doctor De Soto Goes to Africa*. (1993). 34

Stevens, Janet (Illustrator). *Anansi Goes Fishing*. (1993). 26

—— (Reteller and Illustrator). *Coyote Steals the Blanket: A Ute Tale*. (1994). 63

—— (Illustrator). *The Dog Who Had Kittens*. (1992). 35

Stewart, Roger (*see* Harris, Nick)

Stodart, Eleanor. *The Australian Echidna*. (1992). 4

Stover, Jill. *Alamo Across Texas*. (1994). 26

Strasser, Todd (adapted from his film). *Honey, I Blew Up the Kid*. (1993). 86

Suchomski, Stef (Illustrator). *Planes of the Aces: A Three-Dimensional Collection of the Most Famous Aircraft in the World*. (1994). 13

Sullivan, George. *In-Line Skating: A Complete Guide for Beginners*. (1994). 87

——. *Sluggers! Twenty-Seven of Baseball's Greatest*. (1992). 96

——. *Unsolved! Famous Real-Life Mysteries*. (1993). 98

Sweet, Melissa (Illustrator). *Rosie's Baby Tooth*. (1992). 48

Tan, Amy. *The Moon Lady*. (1993). 73

Taylor, Barbara (*see* Cash, Terry)

Teague, Mark. *Frog Medicine*. (1992). 38

Terban, Marvin. *Hey, Hay! A Wagonful of Funny Homonym Riddles*. (1992). 8

Thaler, Mike. *Seven Little Hippos*. (1992). 50–51

Thiesing, Lisa (Illustrator). *Pudmuddles*. (1994). 47

Title Index

Big Pumpkin. Erica Silverman. (1993). 18

Bingo. Beth Goodman (Adapter). (1992). 62

Birds: A First Discovery Book. Gallimard Jeunesse, Claude Delafosse, and René Mettler (Creators). (1994). 4

The Boy Who Sailed with Columbus. Michael Foreman. (1993). 63

Brown Bear, Brown Bear, What Do You See? (25th Anniversary Edition). Bill Martin, Jr. (1993). 31

Bully for You, Teddy Roosevelt! Jean Fritz. (1992). 82

Calico Cows. Arlene Dubanevich. (1994). 31

Castles: A First Discovery Book. Gallimard Jeunesse, Claude Delafosse, C. Millet, and D. Millet (Creators). (1994). 31

Chicken Sunday. Patricia Polacco. (1993). 4

The Children's Animal Atlas. David Lambert. (1993). 5

Children's Classics to Read Aloud. Edward Blishen (Selector). (1993). 6

The Children's Space Atlas. Robin Kerrod. (1993). 63

Christmas in July. Arthur Yorinks. (1992). 6

The Christmas Witch. Steven Kellogg. (1993). 31

Christopher Columbus: From Vision to Voyage. Joan Anderson. (1992). 32

Cinderella Penguin. Janet Perlman (Reteller). (1994). 32

Cinderella. William Wegman with Carole Kismaric and Marvin Heiferman (Retellers). (1994). 6

Civil War! America Becomes One Nation. James I. Robertson, Jr. (1993). 83

Clifford, We Love You. Norman Bridwell. (1992). 32

Coast to Coast. Betsy Byars. (1993). 83

The Courage of Magic Johnson. Peter Pascarelli. (1993). 83

Coyote Steals the Blanket: A Ute Tale. Janet Stevens (Reteller). (1994). 63

Cranberries. William Jaspersohn. (1992). 32

Crosstown. Kathryn Makris. (1994). 83

Custer. Deborah King. (1993). 63

The Cut-Ups Crack Up. James Marshall. (1993). 18

Dad's Dinosaur Day. Diane Dawson Hearn. (1994). 33

David Robinson: NBA Super Center. Bill Gutman. (1994). 64

Dear Mr. Blueberry. Simon James. (1992). 33

Diane Goode's Book of Silly Stories & Songs. Illustrated by Diane Goode. (1993). 33

Did You Hear About Amber? Surviving 16 #1. Cherie Bennett. (1994). 83–84

Die For Me. Carol Gorman. (1993). 64

Dinosaurs at the Supermarket. Lindsay Camp. (1994). 33

Dinostory. Michaela Morgan. (1992). 34

Discovering Christopher Columbus: How History Is Invented. Kathy Pelta. (1992). 64

Do Fishes Get Thirsty? Questions Answered by the New England Aquarium. Les Kaufman and the staff of the New England Aquarium. (1992). 84

Doctor De Soto Goes to Africa. William Steig. (1993). 34

The Dog Who Found Christmas. Linda Jennings. (1994). 35

The Dog Who Had Kittens. Polly Robertus. (1992). 35

Dogs Don't Tell Jokes. Louis Sachar. (1992). 84

Dogs Don't Wear Sneakers. Laura Numeroff. (1994). 35

Dogteam. Gary Paulsen. (1994). 64

Don't Blink Now! Capturing the Hidden World of Sea Creatures. Ann Downer. (1992). 84

Don't Read This Book, Whatever You Do! More Poems About School. Kalli Dakos. (1994). 65

Don't Wake Up Mama! Another Five Little Monkeys Story. Eileen Christelow. (1993). 35

Dragon's Fat Cat. Dave Pilkey. (1993). 36

Draw Me a Star. Eric Carle. (1993). 19

The Earth and Sky. Jean-Pierre Verdet. (1993). 65

Earthquake in the Third Grade. Laurie Myers. (1994). 36

Earthquake. Christopher Lampton. (1992). 65

The Easter Egg Farm. Mary Jane Auch. (1993). 36

Easy to See Why. Fred Gwynne. (1994). 19

Elvira. Margaret Shannon. (1994). 36–37

Exploring the Bismarck: The Real-Life Quest to Find Hitler's Greatest Battleship. Robert D. Ballard. (1992). 84–85

Eyewitness Science: Light. David Burnie. (1993). 85

Eyewitness Science: Matter. Christopher Cooper. (1993). 85

Ezra in Pursuit: The Great Maze Chase. Rosalyn Schanzer. (1994). 37

Finding Buck McHenry. Alfred Slote. (1992). 85

Five Little Monkeys Sitting in a Tree. Eileen Christelow. (1992). 19

For Laughing Out Loud: Poems to Tickle Your Funnybone. Jack Prelutsky (Selector). (1992). 37

Fourth Grade Rats. Jerry Spineli. (1992). 65

Fritz and the Mess Fairy. Rosemary Wells. (1992). 38

Frog Medicine. Mark Teague. (1992). 38

The Frog Prince Continued. Jon Scieszka. (1992). 6

From Sea to Shining Sea: A Treasury of American Folklore and Folk Songs. Amy L. Cohn (Compiler). (1994). 7

George Washington's Mother. Jean Fritz. (1993). 38

George Washington: The Man Who Would Not Be King. Stephen Krensky. (1992). 66

The Ghost of Popcorn Hill. Betty Ren Wright. (1994). 66

Ghost Stories. Robert Westall (Compiler). (1994). 85

The Giant Book of the Mummy. Rosalie David. (1994). 66

The Giant Zucchini. Catherine Siracusa. (1994). 20

The Giver. Lois Lowry. (1994). 86

Go Away, Big Green Monster! Ed Emberley. (1994). 38

Go Hang a Salami! I'm a Lasagna Hog! and Other Palindromes. Jon Agee. (1993). 66

Gobble! The Complete Book of Thanksgiving Words. Lynda Graham-Barber. (1992). 7

Goldilocks and the Three Bears. Jonathan Langley (Reteller). (1994). 39

Gonna Sing My Head Off! Kathleen Krull (Collector and arranger). (1993). 7

Good Days, Bad Days: An Official NFL Book. Tom Barnidge (Editor). (1993). 7

Goodbye, Vietnam. Gloria Whelan. (1993). 67

Granny Greenteeth and the Noise in the Night. Kenn Compton and Joanne Compton. (1994). 39

Green Wilma. Tedd Arnold. (1994). 39

The Grumpalump. Sarah Hayes. (1992). 39

Hakeem Olajuwon: Tower of Power. George R. Rekela. (1994). 86

The Happy Hippopotami. Bill Martin, Jr. (1992). 20

Happy Thanksgiving Rebus. David A. Adler. (1992). 21

Hector's New Sneakers. Amanda Vesey. (1994). 39

Henry's Wild Morning. Margaret Greaves. (1992). 40

Hey, Hay! A Wagonful of Funny Homonym Riddles. Marvin Terban. (1992). 8

Hidden Pictures. Linda Bolton. (1994). 8

Hiding Out: Camouflage in the Wild. James Martin. (1994). 8

The Holiday Handwriting School. Robin Pulver. (1992). 40

Honey, I Blew Up the Kid. Adapted from the film by Todd Strasser. (1993). 86

How Do You Say It Today, Jesse Bear? Nancy White Carlstrom. (1993). 21

How Giraffe Got Such a Long Neck...And Why Rhino Is So Grumpy. Michael Rosen (Reteller). (1994). 40

How on Earth Do We Recycle Paper? Helen Jill Fletcher (crafts) and Seli Groves (text). (1993). 67

How to Be Cool in the Third Grade. Betsy Duffey. (1994). 67

I Am Really a Princess. Carol Diggory Shields. (1994). 8

I Have a Dream: The Life and Words of Martin Luther King, Jr. Jim Haskins. (1993). 87

If Dinosaurs Came to Town. Dom Mansell. (1992). 22

If You Give a Moose a Muffin. Laura Joffe Numeroff. (1992). 40

In a Cabin in a Wood. Darcie McNally (Adaptor). (1992). 22

In the Tall, Tall Grass. Denise Fleming. (1992). 22

In-Line Skating: A Complete Guide for Beginners. George Sullivan. (1994). 87

Incredible Cross-Sections. Richard Platt. (1993). 8–9

Insect Attack. Christopher Lampton. (1993). 67

Inside Story: The Latest News About Your Body. Mike Lambourne. (1993). 68

Inside the Whale and Other Animals. Illustrated by Ted Dewan. Text by Steve Parker. (1993). 41

Inventions: Inventors & Ingenious Ideas. Peter Turvey. (1993). 68

It Happened in America: True Stories from the Fifty States. Lila Perl. (1993). 87–88

It Was a Dark and Stormy Night. Keith Moseley. (1992). 9

Jack and the Beanstalk. Steven Kellogg (Reteller). (1992). 9

Jane Yolen's Mother Goose Songbook. Jane Yolen (Selector and editor). (1993). 9

Jeremy's Tail. Duncan Ball. (1992). 41

Jesse Owens: Olympic Star. Patricia and Fredrick McKissack. (1993). 68

Jingle the Christmas Clown. Tomie dePaola. (1993). 41

A Job for Wittilda. Caralyn Buehner. (1994). 41

John F. Kennedy: Young People's President. Catherine Corley Anderson. (1992). 42

The Jolly Christmas Postman. Janet and Allan Ahlberg. (1992). 88

The Jungle Book. Rudyard Kipling. (1992). 88

King of the Playground. Phyllis Reynolds Naylor. (1992). 42

The Kingfisher Children's Encyclopedia. John Paton (Editor). (1993). 9

The Kingfisher Illustrated Encyclopedia of Animals. Michael Chinery (Editor). (1993). 88

Kirby Puckett: Fan Favorite. Ann Bauleke. (1994). 88

The Kite That Braved Old Orchard Beach. X.J. Kennedy. (1992). 68

Knock! Knock! Colin and Jacqui Hawkins. (1992). 10

Kriss Kross Krazy! Anne Raso. (1993). 89

Kristi Yamaguchi: Artist on Ice. Shiobhan Donohue. (1994). 89

L. Frank Baum: Royal Historian of Oz. Angelica Shirley Carpenter and Jean Shirley. (1993). 90

The Last Princess: The Story of Princess Ka'iulani of Hawai'i. Fay Stanley. (1992). 69

Letting Swift River Go. Jane Yolen. (1993). 90

The Los Angeles Riots: America's Cities in Crisis. John Salak. (1994). 90

The Lost Children. Paul Goble. (1994). 69

Macmillan Animal Encyclopedia for Children. Roger Few. (1992). 69

The Magic School Bus on the Ocean Floor. Joanna Cole. (1993). 69

The Magic: Earvin Johnson. Bill Morgan. (1993). 91

Magnification. Beth B. Norden and Lynette Ruschak. (1994). 70

Make a Splash! Care About the Ocean. Thompson Yardley. (1993). 42

Make Four Million Dollar$ by Next Thur$day! Stephen Manes. (1992). 70

Making Books: A Step-By-Step Guide to Your Own Publishing. Gillian Chapman and Pam Robson. (1993). 10

Making Tracks: A Slide-and-See Book. Stephen Savage. (1993). 10

Malcolm X: Black Rage. David Collins. (1993). 91

Mama, Let's Dance. Patricia Hermes. (1992). 92

The Man Behind the Magic: The Story of Walt Disney. Katherine and Richard Greene. (1992). 10

Manatee: On Location. Kathy Darling. (1992). 70

Martha Speaks. Susan Meddaugh. (1993). 11

Matthew's Dream. Leo Lionni. (1992). 22

Max's Dragon Shirt. Rosemary Wells. (1992). 42

Meet Addy. Connie Porter. (1994). 70

Meet Tricky Coyote! Gretchen Will Mayo (Reteller). (1994). 70

Mind Twisters. Godfrey Hall. (1993). 71

Mission from Mount Yoda. Star Wars #4. Paul Davids and Hollace Davids. (1994). 92

Mistakes That Worked. Charlotte Foltz Jones. (1992). 11

Mona the Brilliant. Sonia Holleyman. (1994). 43

Mona the Vampire. Sonia Holleyman. (1992). 43

Monkey Soup. Louis Sachar. (1993). 22

Monster Mama. Liz Rosenberg. (1994). 12

The Moon Clock. Matt Faulkner. (1992). 43

The Moon Lady. Amy Tan. (1993). 73

The Moon of the Alligators. Jean Craighead George. (1992). 72

The Moon of the Gray Wolves. Jean Craighead George. (1992). 73

The Moon of the Mountain Lions. Jean Craighead George. (1992). 73

Moonshiner's Son. Carolyn Reeder. (1994). 92

Mrs. Bretsky's Bakery. R.L. Shafner and Eric Jon Weisberg. (1994). 12

Mrs. Katz and Tush. Patricia Polacco. (1993). 43

Mrs. Wolf. Shen Roddie. (1994). 43
Mucky Moose. Jonathan Allen. (1992). 44
Mummies and Their Mysteries. Charlotte Wilcox. (1994). 73
My Co-Star, My Enemy. Hollywood Wars #1. Ilene Cooper. (1994). 92
My Friend Whale. Simon James. (1992). 23
My Great-Aunt Arizona. Gloria Houston. (1993). 44
My Mother the Cat. Katherine Potter. (1994). 45

Nature's Deadly Creatures: A Pop-Up Exploration. Frances Jones. (1993). 12
Nightjohn. Gary Paulsen. (1994). 93
Nine O'Clock Lullaby. Marilyn Singer. (1992). 74
No Milk! Jennifer A. Ericsson. (1994). 45
No Plain Pets! Marc Ian Barasch. (1992). 45
Not the Piano, Mrs. Medley! Evan Levine. (1992). 12
Now Everybody Really Hates Me. Jane Read Martin and Patricia Marx.
    (1994). 45

Of Swans, Sugarplums, and Satin Sippers: Ballet Stories for Children.
    Violette Verdy. (1992). 74
Old Black Fly. Jim Aylesworth. (1993). 12–13
The Old Ladies Who Liked Cats. Carol Greene. (1992). 13
On the Tracks of Dinosaurs: A Study of Dinosaur Footprints. James O.
    Farlow. (1992). 94
One Hundred Hungry Ants. Elinor J. Pinczes. (1994). 46
175 Amazing Nature Experiments. Rosie Harlow and Gareth Morgan.
    (1993). 13
175 More Science Experiments to Amuse and Amaze Your Friends. Terry
    Cash, Steve Parker, and Barbara Taylor. (1992). 74
One World. Michael Foreman. (1992). 74
Our Solar System. Seymour Simon. (1993). 75

The Paper Bag Prince. Colin Thompson. (1993). 46
Paper Magic: Creating Fantasies and Performing Tricks with Paper .
    Ormond McGill. (1993). 75
Parents in the Pigpen, Pigs in the Tub. Amy Ehrlich. (1994). 13
Pearl Harbor! Wallace B. Black and Jean F. Blashfield. (1992). 75
Peeping Beauty. Mary Jane Auch. (1994). 46
People in Art. Anthea Peppin. (1993). 94
Pets of the Presidents. Janet Caulkins. (1993). 46
Piggies. Don Wood and Audrey Wood. (1992). 23
Pigs Aplenty, Pigs Galore! David McPhail. (1994). 46–47
*Planes of the Aces: A Three-Dimensional Collection of the Most Famous
    Aircraft in the World.* Joan Bowden. (1994). 13

Polar Bear, Polar Bear, What Do You Hear? Bill Martin, Jr. (1992). 47
Pudmuddles. Carol Beach York. (1994). 47

The Rainbow Fish. Marcus Pfister. J. Alison James (Translater). (1993). 48
The Random House Book of How Things Were Built. David J. Brown.
  (1993). 75
Rats on the Range and Other Stories. James Marshall. (1994). 48
The Rebellious Alphabet. Jorge Diaz. (1994). 76
Rising Voices: Writings of Young Native Americans. Arlene B. Hirshfelder
  and Beverly R. Singer (Selectors). (1993). 94
The River. Gary Paulsen. (1992). 76
A River Ran Wild: An Environmental History. Lynne Cherry. (1993). 76
Rosa Parks: My Story. Rosa Parks with Jim Haskins. (1993). 94
Roseanne Arnold: Comedy's Queen Bee. Katherine E. Krohn. (1994). 95
Rosie's Baby Tooth. Maryann Macdonald. (1992). 48
Ruby the Copycat. Peggy Rathmann. (1992). 48
Rumpelstiltskin. Jonathan Langley (Reteller). (1993). 48–49

Sam's Surprise. David Pilham. (1993). 49
*Saving Endangered Mammals: A Field Guide to Some of the Earth's Rarest
  Animals.* Thane Maynard. (1993). 95
Scary Stories 3: More Tales to Chill Your Bones. Alvin Schwartz (Collector
  and reteller). (1992). 95
Sea Squares. Joy N. Hulme. (1992). 50
The Secrets of Vesuvius: Exploring the Mysteries of an Ancient Buried City.
  Sara C. Bisel. (1992). 95
Seven Blind Mice. Ed Young. (1993). 23
Seven Little Hippos. Mike Thaler. (1992). 50–51
Shadow Theater: Games and Projects. Denny Robson and Vanessa Bailey.
  (1992). 76
Sheep in a Shop. Nancy Shaw. (1992). 23–24
Sheep Out To Eat. Nancy Shaw. (1993). 24
Ships: Sailors and the Sea. Richard Humble. (1992). 96
Siegfried. Diane Stanley. (1992). 51
The Sierra Club Book of Great Mammals. Linsay Knight. (1993). 96
The Sierra Club Book of Weatherwisdom. Vicki McVey. (1992). 96
Silly Sally. Audrey Wood. (1993). 51
Slombo the Gross. Rodney A. Greenblat. (1994). 52
Sluggers! Twenty-Seven of Baseball's Greatest. George Sullivan. (1992). 96
Smart Dog. Ralph Leemis. (1994). 52
Some Birthday! Patricia Polacco. (1992). 52
Somebody Catch My Homework. David L. Harrison. (1994). 14
Somebody Loves You, Mr. Hatch. Eileen Spinelli. (1992). 14

Walt Disney's Alice's Tea Party. Lyn Calder. (1993). 79

Walt Disney's Mickey and the Beanstalk. Teddy Slater (Reteller). (1994). 55

Water's Way. Lisa Westberg Peters. (1992). 79

Water. François Michel (Paper engineer). (1994). 56

Way Out West Lives a Coyote Named Frank. Jillian Lund. (1994). 57

Westward Ho Ho Ho! Jokes from the Wild West. Victoria Hartman. (1993). 80

Whales. Gail Gibbons. (1992). 16

Whales: A First Discovery Book. Gallimard Jeunesse, Claude Delafosse, Ute Fuhr, and Raoul Sautai (Creators). (1994). 57

What Daddy Did. Neal Shusterman. (1992). 98

What's on the Menu? Food Poems. Bobbye Goldstein (Selector). (1993). 80

When I Was Little: A Four-Year-Old's Memoir of Her Youth. Jamie Lee Curtis. (1994). 25

When I Was Your Age. Ken Adams. (1992). 16

Where on Earth: A Geografunny Guide to the Globe. Paul Rosenthal. (1993). 80

Where's That Bus? Eileen Browne. (1992). 57

Who Are You? John Schindel. (1992). 58

Widow's Broom. Chris Van Allsburg. (1993). 59

Willow Pattern Story. Allan Drummond. (1993). 16

Wind in the Long Grass: A Collection of Haiku. William J. Higginson (Editor). (1992). 17

Window on the Deep: Adventures of Underwater Explorer Sylvia Earle. Andrea Conley. (1992). 17

Wings. Jane Yolen. (1992). 80

Wonders of Science. Melvin Berger. (1992). 81

Worm's Eye View: Make Your Own Wildlife Refuge. Kipchak Johnson. (1992). 81

The Worst Day I Ever Had. Fred McMane and Cathrine Wolf. (1992). 98

The Wretched Stone. Chris Van Allsburg. (1992). 81

Yo, Hungry Wolf! David Vozar. (1994). 59

A Young Painter: The Life and Paintings of Wang Yan—China's Extraordinary Young Artist. Zheng Zhensun and Alice Low. (1992). 17